MW01622105

Delicious
by Design
30 YEARS / 30 RECIPES

This book is dedicated to

Lynn Ann Lubitz

sister, friend,
fellow cooking enthusiast,
and eternal optimist

PUBLISHED BY AURAS CUSTOM PUBLISHING
8435 GEORGIA AVENUE
SILVER SPRING, MARYLAND 20910

THIS BOOK IS TYPESET IN H&FJ MERCURY,
MUSEO SANS AND MUSEO SLAB

PRINTED IN CANADA

ISBN 978-0-578-09232-4

LIBRARY OF CONGRESS CONTROL NUMBER: 2011917801

Delicious by Design

30 YEARS / 30 RECIPES

ROBERT SUGAR

Photography | Renée Comet
Styling | Lisa Cherkasky

Thomas -
Happy Holidays!!!
Renée

AURAS DESIGN

CONTENTS

Main Dishes

Starters, Sides, Spices, and Sauces

About AURAS

When we began to contemplate how we were going to mark the 30th anniversary of AURAS Design, our idea was to produce a book of our past graphic design work. But, really, who wants to look at that more than once? Not that we aren't proud of the work we've done (see the samples on page 74), but we wanted to create something that people would actually enjoy using and refer to now and again.

Then, an obvious idea sprung to mind: let's make a cookbook. After all, cooking is a lot like designing. There's a lot of thought put into the ingredients; it takes technique and tools to produce excellent work; and if everything works just right, the end result is pretty tasty.

Maybe that's why I have enjoyed cooking since I was old enough to hold a spatula. In college, with nothing more than a hot plate and toaster oven, I learned how to prepare meals. AURAS has produced work for hundreds of clients over the last three decades, but now, here's an opportunity to see what we might have created if things had gone just a bit differently.

In fact, the lure of opening a restaurant has always been a siren call for me. I think I have mentioned it so many times that my more sensible other half, Helen Rea, merely goes "Whoop-whoop"—indicating the alarm bells that should be going off in my head. Restaurants, like Broadway shows and Internet start-ups, are a high-risk long shot. They make running a design studio seem like a sensible business—even these days.

Food has always been an important part of celebration at AURAS. For years, our holiday parties have been renowned for the great food—mostly cooked by us. Our holiday staff retreats were always chosen for the quality of the food, whether it was a limo trip to the Inn at Little Washington or an overnight stay at l'Auberge Provençal. We have always kept ourselves caffeinated and content by stocking the finest foodstuffs for everyone to enjoy.

When our studio was on Kalorama Road, many mornings on the way to work I would stop by Posin's, the late, lamented D.C. Jewish supermarket, and buy donuts, cupcakes and freshly made rye bread for the studio. The bread was too warm to bag and too delicious not to steal the crusty end slices as I headed down 13th Street.

Having a full kitchen has always been an important part of the plan, wherever our studio has been. The long-time people at AURAS warn newcomers about "The AURAS Ten"—the weight that is bound to be put on from the abundance of good stuff around the shop. On summer afternoons at the Kalorama studio, taking a break for former employee Marty Ittner's guacamole was a welcome treat; on snow days, I often make a hearty vegetable soup to entice the crew to brave the elements. And all year long there is coffee, whether an afternoon cappuccino break or simply a strong, bracing cup of Peet's, freshly ground and shipped directly to the studio. For many new employees, the first challenge of working at AURAS was learning to appreciate that super-strong brew. If nothing else, AURAS was way ahead of the coffee-crazed curve.

So, think of *Delicious by Design* as the restaurant that never was. Within these pages are recipes that have been prepared and tweaked over the years. They are heavy on comfort and powerful in taste. And in the back, we've allowed ourselves a few pages for a history of our studio and some examples of AURAS design work.

Renée Comet was excited to become part of this project and brought Lisa Cherkasky along to prepare and style the food. Together we mapped out a simple strategy: every picture should look so tasty that readers might be inclined to lick the page—that was the extent of the art direction. I have always believed that you should let talented people do what they do best and try to stay out of the way.

We'd like to know what you think of this book—especially how you like the recipes—and give you a chance to see some behind-the-scenes action at the photo shoot—plus a few recipes that didn't make it into the book. Check out www.aurascookbook.com.

Bon appétit! —RS

USING BONELESS SHORT RIBS makes this dish easier to prepare by eliminating much of the unwanted fat and connective tissue—a good trade-off for losing the bones. Since the bones add richness to the braising liquid, we add gelatin to achieve the same effect, similar to adding demi-glace, which is nice if you have it—but you probably don't.

The ribs are braised in a Dutch oven that's placed in the oven, where the heat cooks more evenly and avoids the danger of burning the pot bottom. **Le Creuset** enameled cast-iron cookware is perfect for this job, and you'll find it can be the hardest working pot in your cooking arsenal.

The braising liquid absorbs the flavors from the spices and aromatics and the sweetness from the carrots. The vegetal additions are all discarded near the end, leaving the rich stock. The tomato and anchovy pastes raise the *umami* quotient of the meat without adding any distinctive flavor of their own.

Some people can't imagine short ribs without the braised vegetables, so a variation on this recipe calls for more carrots cut into 1-inch pieces, a small onion sliced pole-to-pole, and 4 Yukon Gold potatoes peeled and cut into 1-inch chunks—all added, with the meat, to the braising liquid after it has been strained and returned to the pot. The additional time cooks the new vegetables without making them overly soft.

Braised Short Ribs in Red Wine

SERVES 6

- **3 lbs** boneless short ribs
- **3 Tbs** olive or other vegetable oil
- **1** large onion, cut into 1/2-inch pieces pole-to-pole
- **4** garlic cloves, chopped fine
- **3** carrots, chopped into 1-inch dice
- **1 Tbs** fresh thyme (about 2 stalks)
- **1 Tbs** fresh rosemary (5-inch stalk)
- **1** bottle red wine (preferably a full-bodied Cabernet)
- **2 Tbs** tomato paste
- **1 tsp** anchovy paste
- **1/2** package plain gelatin

Set oven to 400°. Pat short rib pieces dry, remove any shreds of fat on meat. On stovetop, heat 2 tablespoons oil in an 8-quart Dutch oven set over medium-high heat until just smoking. Sear short ribs in two batches, patiently waiting for each side to brown, about 8 minutes total for each piece. Each side should form a deep brown sear. Remove the first batch to a plate. Add the third tablespoon of oil and the second batch of short ribs. When these are done, remove to the plate too.

Prepare vegetables while the ribs are browning. Add the onions and carrots to the now-empty pot and sauté until onions are softened, about 2 minutes. Add garlic and sauté until fragrant, about 1 minute. Add thyme and rosemary stalks.

Return short ribs to pot along with any juices. Stir to combine. Add bottle of red wine, and use a wooden spoon to scrape any *fond* from the bottom of the pot while deglazing. The wine should cover the short ribs. If it doesn't, add water until ribs are just covered. Allow liquid to begin to boil and take off heat. Add tomato paste and anchovy paste; stir in. Cover Dutch oven with lid and place in oven to cook for 2 hours or until meat is very tender.

Remove pot from oven. The braising liquid should be reduced but still somewhat thin. Remove meat from pot with tongs and set aside. Pass remaining contents of pot through a fine strainer or *chinoise*, pressing on solids to extract as much liquid as possible into a large measuring cup. Discard solids. Take a few ounces of the liquid to use for dissolving the gelatin in a small cup. Stir in the powder, let rest for 2 minutes to allow the gelatin to melt, then pour the liquid back into the rest of the stock while stirring. Add liquid and short ribs back into the pot, cover, and replace in oven for another 30 minutes. The liquid will thicken into a smooth sauce.

Not-Macaroni and Cheeses

SERVES 6

- **8 oz** large penne, ziti or similar dried tubular pasta
- **2 Tbs** salt (for pasta water)
- **1 slice** thick-sliced bacon, diced small
- **1 tsp** thyme (or 1 Tbs fresh)
- **1** large shallot, diced fine
- **2** garlic cloves, diced fine
- **4 oz** container of crimini (or baby bella) mushrooms, stems removed, cut into 1/4-inch pieces
- **1 tsp** salt
- **1/4 cup** white wine
- **4 Tbs** all-purpose flour
- **4 Tbs** butter
- **2 cups** chicken stock (homemade or Swanson low sodium)
- **1 cup** heavy cream
- **1 cup** whole milk
- **1** bay leaf
- **4 oz** Cabot Extra Sharp Cheddar (1 cup shredded)
- **4 oz** pepper jack cheese (1 cup shredded)
- **1/4 cup** Parmesan, shredded or grated
- **1/4 cup** bread crumbs

In a 10-inch skillet, add bacon over medium heat and cook until fat renders and bacon begins to brown, about 2 minutes. Add thyme, garlic, and shallots and stir until fragrant, about 1 minute. Add mushrooms and salt; toss to combine; cover skillet. Cook over medium heat until mushrooms render liquid and begin to brown, about 8 minutes. When the liquid is evaporated, deglaze the skillet with white wine, scraping any browned bits from the bottom with a wooden spoon. When liquid evaporates, remove from heat. What's left will be very dark brown.

In a 10-quart pot, bring 4 quarts water to a boil, and add salt; wait for the water to boil again, and then add pasta and stir. Do not add oil to the pasta water. Cook pasta just short of *al dente*, about 11 minutes. The pasta will finish cooking in the oven. Drain pasta and reserve. Allow some liquid to stay with the drained pasta.

Heat chicken stock in microwave or on stove until hot. Mix milk and cream, warm in microwave, but do not allow mixture to boil. Shred cheeses using medium holes on a grater or food processor.

In a 4-quart saucepan, melt butter until froth subsides; add flour and cook *roux* until light tan, about 2 minutes. While whisking, slowly add stock until thickened and bubbling, followed by milk and cream mixture. Stir until the *béchamel* thickens. Add bay leaf and simmer for 10 minutes. Remove leaf and add Cheddar and jack cheeses, stirring until smooth.

Combine pasta and mushroom mixture in a 2-quart baking dish, preferably deep rather than wide. Pour cheese sauce over pasta. There will be a lot of sauce in the dish, so gently tap the dish or slowly stir the pasta to evenly distribute the cheese sauce, getting it into the open tubes. Combine Parmesan and bread crumbs in a bowl. Sprinkle crumb mixture on top.

Place in 350° oven and bake until bubbling and brown on top, about 30 minutes. Let cool 10 minutes before serving.

THE SECRET TO THIS MACARONI AND CHEESE IS NOT TO USE MACARONI, but a larger tubular pasta. This is about as far from Kraft as you can get, and the final result has a combination of familiar creamy goodness with layers of complexity from adding savory elements like mushrooms, bacon, and chicken stock. The dish is almost impossible to stop eating, which is why making it in 10-ounce ramekins instead of one large dish might be a good idea.

The basics of a mac and cheese are here—a *béchamel* sauce with cheeses added and tubular pasta—but like anything well-designed, the delight is in the details. First, we replace elbow macaroni with *penne, rigatoni, ziti* or *mostaccioli*—larger tubes big enough to absorb the sauce on the inside and the outside. Starting with a base of thyme, bacon, shallots, mushrooms, and garlic gives the final dish a distinctive flavor that amplifies the complexity of the two cheeses.

There is plenty of sauce here—1 quart of liquid—but don't be surprised if there is no sauce in the final casserole. The pasta absorbs almost all of it, making each bite that much more delicious.

COOKING A RIB ROAST is as simple a job as any cooking assignment, but like anything else, preparation makes a big difference in the final product. Often the rib roast is offered boneless (sometimes referred to as a Delmonico roast), but bones add to the flavor. It is a simple matter to cut off the bones and, after seasoning the meat, use them to protect the tender meat by reattaching them against the roast with kitchen twine. When the meat is done, simply remove the ribs—which are pretty delicious on their own, especially when cooked on the grill—and then slice the boneless roast any thickness desired.

MAKING FRIENDS WITH A BUTCHER IS THE FIRST STEP. Most supermarket beef is pretty bland. Finding a local butcher you trust at a place that chooses its vendors with care ensures your beef starts out right. Around Silver Spring, we get our meat from Snider's Super Foods, one of the few local groceries still around. Frank, my butcher, is always looking out for me. And spending $8 a pound for a rib roast sure beats spending 50 bucks a pound mail-ordering from Lobels in New York.

THE MOST IMPORTANT TOOL FOR COOKING ROASTS IS A GOOD INSTANT-READ THERMOMETER. It is much better than the kind you stick into the roast and leave in. The best choice is the **Thermapen**, made by Thermoworks. It is a bit pricey, but is useful over a wide range of temperatures—you can use it to measure the temperature of hot oil—and gives a quicker read than any other thermometer. Since a good roast could cost $100, one averted disaster pays for the Thermapen.

THE IDEAL COOKING DEVICE FOR THIS ROAST IS A WEBER GRILL, using indirect heat. Make a fire on one side of the kettle and place an aluminum pan next to the charcoal to catch drippings on the "cool side" of the grill. The meat is placed over the pan, and the bones are used to protect the meat from the hot coals. Adjust the vents to maintain a 400° temperature. After 30 minutes of cooking, add on top of the coals some hickory or applewood chips that have been soaked in water. This creates a 10-minute smoke that will add extra flavor to the roast.

ON THE SUBJECT OF CHARCOAL, avoid briquets, especially the "quick-light" variety. There is no reason for using the noxious chemicals they're saturated with, or lighter fluid, when a charcoal chimney works faster and better. And any kind of briquet contains nearly 50% binder, so half of what you bought doesn't even burn. Instead, buy real hardwood charcoal. It burns hotter, adds a pleasant smoky tinge, and leaves almost no residue in the ash catcher.

Un-Ribbed Roast

SERVES 8

5–6 lb center-cut standing rib roast (three ribs)
2 Tbs kosher salt
2 tsp freshly ground pepper
5 garlic cloves, slivered

Prepare indirect fire in a grill or preheat oven to 400°. Prepare the roast by cutting the bones off the meat just above their tops by slicing parallel to the surface of the roast where they attach. Using a paring knife, make small 1-inch incisions in the surface of the roast at even intervals, and insert a sliver of garlic into each incision. Generously sprinkle kosher salt and pepper over entire roast. Using kitchen twine, tie the bones to underside of the roast from where they were removed, to act as a "tray" for the roast to sit on as it cooks. Place roast in shallow roasting pan to cook in oven, or place directly on grill over a drip pan placed under grill rack on cool side of grill. Covered grill should have vents adjusted to keep temperature at 400°; add more fuel as needed. The roast could take as long as 90 minutes to cook, but start checking the temperature at 45 minutes.

Cook roast until instant-read thermometer registers 110° in center. If cooking on grill, remove lid and sear surface on hot side of grill before removing roast to rest. Remove from heat and let sit for 20 minutes, during which time internal temperature will rise to 130° for medium rare.

After removing string, the roast can be sliced across the grain. The ribs can be cut and served—some people even prefer them.

Super-Slow BBQ Baby-Back Ribs

SERVES 3-4

2 racks baby back ribs
1/4 cup AURAS Spice Mix (recipe at right)
1/4 cup dark brown sugar
1/2 cup ketchup

WET SAUCE

1/2 cup ketchup
1/4 cup brown sugar
1/4 cup apple cider vinegar
1 Tbs AURAS Spice Mix

Rinse and pat ribs dry. Remove membrane on bottom side of ribs by pulling up at one corner and pulling across rack at a low angle against the bones. Using a paring knife, cut 1-inch slits between bones. Mix brown sugar and spice mix until well combined and generously cover ribs on meat side and around edges. Let meat rest for 30 minutes. Heat oven to 180°.

Wrap ribs tightly in heavy-duty foil, meat-side up, and place on baking sheet. Place in center of oven to cook for 4 hours. Do not be tempted to check on them. At the end of the 4 hours, remove ribs from oven and carefully open foil. The ribs should be fork-tender, and there should be juices in the foil. Decant juice to a separator, and remove fat.

Raise oven temperature to 400°. Make wet sauce by cooking ketchup, brown sugar, vinegar, spice mix and reserved rib liquid until it reduces to 1/2 cup. Slather on ribs and return to oven uncovered until ribs become dark bronze, about 15 minutes. Apply additional wet sauce as needed but avoid burning. Remove from oven, slice into individual ribs with sharp knife, and serve with any remaining sauce.

AURAS Spice Mix

MAKES 24 OZ (FITS CONVENIENTLY IN COMMERCIAL BOTTLES)

This all-purpose seasoning works with just about anything. It works with firm-fleshed fish like salmon as well as with beef. With the addition of brown sugar in one-to-one proportions, it also makes a great dry rub on pork.

5 oz table salt, pulsed in spice mill
1 oz pepper
4 oz garlic powder
4 oz onion powder
3 oz paprika
3 oz chile powder
2 oz dried lemon peel
1 oz cumin
3 Tbs allspice
3 Tbs cayenne pepper

Using a coffee grinder to pulverize the table salt into a finer grind will make the mixture more evenly textured, but it isn't necessary. Still, having a dedicated grinder for spices is an inexpensive addition to your kitchen tools.

Savory Spice Blend

MAKES 8 OZ

Create your own blends by grinding spices together. An inexpensive coffee mill like one from Krups works perfectly as a spice grinder. The following is a savory blend that's tasty on homemade crostini or sprinkled on eggs, roasted meats, or even savory nuts. Add all of this to the grinder and pulse fine; store in an empty 12-ounce spice bottle.

3 oz dry rosemary
3 oz fennel seeds
1 oz celery seed
2 oz dried thyme
1 oz dried oregano
2 oz McCormick Montreal Seasoning

AUTHENTIC BBQ RIBS often nestle in hickory embers for an entire day. This recipe can't match that experience, but comes close. It delivers wonderfully flavorful, tender meat by starting with a dry rub, then long slow cooking, and finishes by building a nice "bark"—the crusty, chewy exterior—with a wet sauce that caramelizes in a hot oven.

The effect can be multiplied by using the same recipe in a smoker. Using some hickory or applewood chips gives the meat an extra layer of flavor and complexity that the oven can't match. Even without a smoker, finishing the ribs on a grill over indirect heat with a handful of soaked hickory chips does a pretty good job of reaching BBQ heaven.

THIS IS AN EASY, ALMOST FOOL-PROOF WAY TO ROAST A CHICKEN, with many of the benefits of butterflying or spatchcock but almost none of the work. The skin protects the delicate flesh from the high temperature, and the bones on the bottom keep the meat from drying out. This technique is a joy for people who love the skin, which is entirely exposed and crisps perfectly. It is nearly impossible to overcook the bird in this manner, but if the skin becomes too dark, place some foil loosely over the bird.

BEFORE FLATTENING, DRY-SALT FOR AN HOUR by spreading a generous amount of salt on and in the bird. This helps the meat stay moist and doesn't lend much saltiness. The herb butter also helps the flesh stay moist, so it's important to get it under the skin of the breast and work it around.

Serving the roasted chicken family style allows people to pick at the carcass to find the small morsels of meat in the back of the bird that are usually missed, a messy experience that adds to the tasty fun of serving this flattened chicken.

Flat-Roast Chicken

SERVES 3-4

4 lbs	kosher or free-range roasting chicken such as Bell & Evans
4 Tbs	kosher salt
3 Tbs	butter
1 Tbs	herbes de Provence
to taste	AURAS Spice Mix (page 9)

Prepare chicken by removing any packed organs, rinsing thoroughly, and patting dry. Generously sprinkle kosher salt on bird, rubbing into cavity and skin. Refrigerate for 1 hour.

After bird has rested, rinse away the salt mixture and pat dry. Position the chicken with the cavity facing you and use a pair of kitchen shears to cut horizontally through the rib bones below the breasts, from the cavity toward the front on both sides. Do not cut all the way through; the breasts should still be attached by cartilage and skin at the front. Swing the entire breast section up from the rear to the front, like opening the hood of a car, exposing the ribcage and backbone of the bird. Sprinkle generously with kosher salt and pepper, or use spice mix. Flip the bird over and flatten with the heel of your hand at the top of the breasts. The meat and skin will now all be on the top, and the bird will be flattened. Tuck wings under body.

Combine the herbes de Provence and the butter to make an herb-butter mixture. Using your fingers to work the skin loose from the meat, spread half the butter under the skin of the breast. Work the rest into the skin of the bird, then apply spice mix generously over the entire skin.

Preheat oven to 400°, or prepare a Weber grill for indirect heat (bank coals to one side of grill). If roasting, place flattened chicken on a rack in a rimmed baking sheet lined with heavy-duty foil curled at the edges to contain juices. If grilling, form foil into a container shape or use an aluminum tray placed under the grill rack beside banked coals to catch the drippings. Place chicken on rack above foil.

Cook until temperature at the thigh reads 170° and juices are clear, 45 minutes to 1 hour. Let bird rest for 10 minutes. Serve on large platter, pouring accumulated juices over bird.

Chicken Parmesan

SERVES 4

- **4** split skinless, boneless chicken breasts (or 4 skinless, boneless thighs)
- **1/2 cup** all-purpose flour
- **1/4 cup** AURAS Spice Mix (page 9)
- **1** egg, beaten with a few tablespoons of water
- **1/2 cup** seasoned bread crumbs
- **1/2 cup** Parmesan, grated
- **1 cup** vegetable oil
- **8 oz** fresh mozzarella

Preheat oven to 400°. Trim edges of breasts, removing thin, small bits of meat and fat. Flip each breast over to expose underside and tenderloin. Use a sharp paring or boning knife to gently cut the tender away from center of breast, leaving it attached at the outside. (If tenders come off, make them separate small pieces.) Remove the thin piece of tendon if necessary. Starting at the center of the breast and cutting parallel to its length, make a horizontal cut toward the outside of the thickest part to butterfly the breast meat. The tender and the flap open like a book from the center of the breast. The result will be a large, nearly uniform piece of chicken. Trim any hanging pieces.

Bread in three steps by combining flour and spice mix in one deep bowl, adding egg to a second bowl, and combining bread crumbs and Parmesan in a third. Dredge chicken in flour mixture, covering entire surface; dip in egg to coat, and then dredge in bread crumbs, tossing to coat completely. Place breaded chicken cutlet on foil and repeat with remaining pieces. Let dry 15 minutes.

Using a 12-inch nonstick skillet, heat oil to shimmering, about 360°. Add cutlets three at a time and fry to an even light brown, about 3 minutes each side. Drain on paper towels.

Place chicken onto a wire rack inserted on a foil-lined, rimmed baking sheet. Ladle 1/4 cup of Simple Marinara sauce over each cutlet. Cut mozzarella into 1/2-inch-thick disks. Center a disk on each piece of chicken and place in oven. Cook until mozzarella is melted, bubbly, and starting to brown, about 10 minutes. Serve immediately.

Simple Marinara

SERVES 6

- **1/4 cup** olive oil
- **1** medium onion, diced fine
- **3** garlic cloves, minced
- **1 Tbs** oregano
- **1/2 Tbs** basil
- **1/2 tsp** rosemary
- **1/2 tsp** sage
- **1** 20-ounce can tomato puree (preferably San Marzano, without calcium chloride added)
- **1** small (4-ounce) can tomato paste
- **1/2 tsp** salt
- **1 Tbs** sugar
- **2 Tbs** balsamic vinegar

Heat oil to shimmering in 4-quart saucepan. Add onion and cook until very soft but not brown. Add minced garlic and stir. Cook until fragrant, about 1 minute. Add remaining ingredients and stir to combine. Reduce heat to medium and cook covered for 30 minutes until sauce thickens and bubbles, stirring occasionally.

THIS CHICKEN PARMESAN RECIPE AVOIDS MANY OF THE CLICHÉS. Instead of pounding the meat thin, careful (but easy-to-do) butterflying makes a tender, thin cutlet that actually tastes like chicken. Cheese in the breading keeps the meat tender while adding a nutty flavor. Finally, lots of fresh mozzarella over a fresh marinara completes the dish.

The best presentation of this dish relies on careful preparation of the cutlet. Trim off the ends and any ragged pieces, even if there is a lot of waste. Don't worry if the tenders come off the breast. They can even be cut off deliberately and cooked separately. The tenders make a great snack while waiting for the cheese to melt.

Frying the chicken cutlets seals in the juices, so be careful to entirely coat each piece with breading. Drying them for 15 minutes lets them cook evenly with less splattering. The cutlets will not be cooked through after frying (although the tenders will be, if you make them separately). Allowing the cutlets to finish in the oven also keeps them juicy.

Finally, upping the flavor in this dish is as simple as changing out the chicken parts. Using skinless, boneless thighs instead of breast meat is certainly unorthodox, but the tastiness of the entire dish is a worthwhile trade-off for the additional fattiness of the dark meat.

STEAKHOUSES USE SALAMANDERS—basically super-hot broilers—to give their steaks a crispy crust and a juicy interior, but nothing beats cooking beef on a Weber grill. The real restaurant cooking secret is, for thick pieces of steak, searing the surface to make the classic crosshatch, and then finishing in the oven to the desired degree of doneness.

MAKE NO MISTAKE, THE SECRET TO A GREAT STEAK STARTS WITH A GREAT PIECE OF MEAT—A THICK PIECE. There's a reason the signature steak at most great steakhouses is the Porterhouse-for-Two. That's at least a 2-inch-thick combination of New York strip and filet mignon in one steak with a big bone in between that adds flavor.

Grilling a 3-pound piece of meat is a two-step process of searing the meat on a super hot grate, then moving the steak away from the heat to finish interior cooking.

Most restaurants buy prime-grade meat, and many will promote their steaks as aged. But there are actually two kinds of aging—wet and dry. Most loins (the primal cut that the porterhouse is butchered from) are wet-aged for a few weeks, but real enhanced flavor comes from dry-aging the meat—allowing it to rest exposed in a cold, dry environment. The meat actually changes, becoming more tender and acquiring a kind of nutty flavor as moisture (up to 15%) is removed and enzymes in the meat work their magic.

THERE ARE TWO WAYS TO GET THE ADVANTAGES OF DRY AGING AT HOME. One technique is to put the steak in an uncovered plastic container, raising it off the bottom and loosely covering it with cheesecloth. Let the steak sit in the coldest part of the refrigerator for 3 days, rewrapping the meat periodically with the same cloth. The surface will lose its bright red color as the meat loses some moisture, but that won't matter once it is seared. Most refrigerators are too humid to do a great job desiccating the meat, but 3 days won't hurt it, either.

A second technique suggested by *Cook's Illustrated* involves slowly heating the steak in a 200° oven until the internal temperature reaches 90°, about 20 minutes (vigilance with a thermometer is a must). The slow cooking of the meat imitates the effects of aging, and then a quick finish on a hot grill brings the meat to the desired doneness with a nice crust.

At Bourbon Steak, Michael Mina's steakhouse, his meat is actually poached *sous vide* style in butter, and then seared over mesquite open flames.

Perfect Steak

SERVES 4

2–3 lbs	porterhouse
1 Tbs	olive oil
2 Tbs	kosher salt
2 Tbs	freshly ground pepper

Bring steak to room temperature. Rub with oil and sprinkle really generously with kosher salt and pepper to cover both sides and the edges. Allow to rest for 30 minutes.

Prepare coals in a Weber grill by completely filling a charcoal chimney with hardwood charcoal and lighting according to directions. When flames come from top of chimney, empty and evenly spread coals onto one side of kettle, leaving other side empty. Place grate on grill and allow to get very hot, about 6-8 minutes.

Place steak over one end of coals. Don't move for 2 minutes. Flip steak over to other end of coals, and leave for 2 minutes. Rotate steak 90 degrees and flip back to original location. Leave for 1 minute. This should sear the steak surface and add nice grill marks. If coals flare up, put lid on the grill. Move steak away from coals, placing the fatty-strip side of the steak nearest the coals. Cover and cook until steak is medium-rare—about 8 minutes or until instant-read thermometer reads 120°. Remove from heat and loosely cover with foil. Allow to rest for at least 5 minutes. Resting the meat is important, because it allows the meat to reabsorb some juices and finish cooking.

Trim meat off bone and cut 1-inch-wide slices perpendicular to center bone. Reposition slices around bone and serve on platter.

Swordfish with Avocado Coulis

SERVES 6

- **2 lbs** swordfish steak, cut 1½ inches thick, skin removed if desired
- **1/4 cup** olive oil
- **2 tsp** ginger
- **1/4 cup** soy sauce
- **2** scallions, chopped
- **1/4 cup** lime juice
- **1 tsp** sugar

Cut swordfish into 6 even pieces, avoiding the dark brown center of the fillet. Create the marinade by combining the rest of the ingredients in a bowl and whisking vigorously. Reserve 1/4 cup. Toss remainder gently with fish and allow to rest, covered at room temperature for 30 minutes, turning fish occasionally. Discard marinade after use, but don't pat fish dry.

Make a charcoal fire in one side of a Weber grill and heat grate until very hot. To prevent sticking, pour oil onto a loosely bunched piece of foil held in long tongs and rub onto the surface of the grill. Immediately add swordfish and cover grill, with lid vents all the way open and cover slightly askew. Cook for 2 minutes; uncover grill; turn swordfish; recover loosely; and cook for 3 more minutes. Uncover again and move fish to cooler side of grill; sprinkle on reserved marinade and cover completely (with vents still open) for 2 more minutes, or until swordfish is tender when pierced and appears slightly puffed.

Plate and add a few tablespoons of Avocado Coulis on top. Serve immediately.

Avocado Coulis

- **2 oz** Major Grey's mango chutney (Crosse & Blackwell brand recommended)
- **1** avocado, cut into small pieces
- **1** tomato, cut into small pieces including seeds
- **1/4** sweet onion finely diced (Vidalia or similar)
- **1/4 cup** lime juice
- **1/8 tsp** salt
- **1/8 tsp** cayenne pepper (optional)

Combine all ingredients in small bowl and toss gently. Let rest in refrigerator for at least 1 hour to let flavors combine.

SWORDFISH BENEFITS FROM THE SAME KIND OF GRILLING AS STEAK. And just like steak, thicker is better for getting a juicy interior and a nice crust. But swordfish is much more lean and benefits from a marinade to both add flavor and help form a crust. This marinade has oil and sugar to help with the crust, as well as flavor enhancers that work perfectly with the Avocado Coulis.

The recipe calls for removal of the skin, but many people find the charred and fatty skin delicious, and it helps retain moisture. So it is not a bad idea to leave the skin on and let people remove it or eat it if they wish.

Major Grey's chutney is a brand name of Crosse & Blackwell, but it's often used generically to refer to all English chutneys. Chutneys are essentially a combination of fruits and their skins marinated with sugar and vinegar. There are lots of recipes for making chutney from scratch, but a bottle from the store is a simpler solution for providing the base to this refreshing coulis.

However, if you want to go totally locavore, substitute 1/4 cup of a peeled and finely diced ripe peach mixed with a tablespoon of apple cider vinegar for the bottled chutney.

The coulis is also great with seared tuna.

Sea Bass in Foil

SERVES 6

MEALS *EN PAPILLOTE* ARE EASY TO PREPARE AND FUN TO SERVE. Although the term means "in paper," aluminum foil works as well as parchment for retaining the steam that cooks the food.

THE SECRET TO SUCCESS IS CUTTING THE VEGETABLES INTO MATCHSTICK JULIENNE SO THEY WILL COOK QUICKLY. Getting them to finish at the same time as the fish is the goal. In a very hot oven in the closed environment of the packet, they'll cook quickly.

You may want to allow diners to carefully open their own pouches and get the first savory whiffs of steam that come from each package.

Although a firm-fleshed fish is ideal for this, there are alternatives that can be interesting and somewhat unexpected. Thinly sliced chicken breast or tenders will cook in foil nicely in about 15 minutes, but to up the flavor, it's best to season the chicken and let it rest for 15 minutes before assembling the packet.

Using a liquor instead of the wine will also amp up the flavor. An anise-flavored apéritif like ouzo, Pernod, or Sambuca will give the fish a subtle licorice finish. Adding a flavored brandy or lemoncello can bring fruity accents to the dish. These additions will really add punch to the juice.

This recipe mates well with a nice rice pilaf that can soak up the juice from the rendered vegetables, wine, and oil. Or, if you want to be a bit more esoteric, try this with a side of quinoa, an ancient grain with a nutty flavor that is a little like couscous in texture.

2 lbs	Chilean sea bass or other firm-fleshed mild fish
2	carrots, matchstick julienned
1	red pepper, matchstick julienned
1	large onion cut pole-to-pole in 1/2-inch slices
1 oz	ginger, peeled and cut into thin pieces
1/4	fennel bulb, cut into 1/4-inch strips
2 Tbs	lemon zest (from 1 lemon) cut into thin strips
18	snap peas, strings removed
6 oz	white wine
6 Tbs	olive oil
1 tsp	herbes de Provence
	kosher salt to taste
	squeeze of fresh lemon juice

Preheat oven to 400°. Chop vegetables and keep each in its own bowl. Arrange 6 pieces of 18×18-inch heavy aluminum foil on a work surface. Divide vegetables evenly among each sheet of foil, piling them in the center of the sheet and positioning so the julienned pieces are all in a lengthwise direction. Pour 1 ounce white wine and squeeze of lemon onto vegetables.

Cut sea bass into 6 pieces and place on top of vegetables. Pour 1 tablespoon of olive oil onto each pile; add a squeeze of lemon juice from half a lemon and a sprinkle of kosher salt and herbes de Provence on top.

Fold the foil around the food, first lengthwise, parallel to the julienned vegetables; fold top edges over each other to seal; fold up each end and pinch against horizontal fold to enclose. Place purses on a baking sheet and put into oven.

Cook for 12 minutes. Remove from oven and let sit a few minutes. Using shears, carefully cut top and one side of each pouch. Slide contents into a bowl or high-rimmed plate, allowing juices to collect in center.

Ultimate Meatloaf

SERVES 8

- **4 lbs** freshly ground chuck
- **2 Tbs** olive oil
- **1** large onion, diced fine
- **1** stalk celery, diced fine
- **4** garlic cloves, minced
- **1 Tbs** tomato paste
- **1/2 Tbs** smoked paprika
- **2 Tbs** Worcestershire sauce
- **2 Tbs** soy sauce
- **1/2 cup** tomato juice
- **10** saltine crackers, crushed
- **1/2** pack unflavored gelatin
- **1/2 cup** chicken stock
- **1** egg
- **2 Tbs** salt
- **1/2 Tbs** mustard

GLAZE

- **1/2 cup** ketchup
- **1/2 cup** brown sugar
- **1/2 cup** apple juice
- **2 Tbs** balsamic vinegar

Preheat oven to 375°. In a 10-inch skillet heat oil until shimmering. Add onion and celery, and sauté until onions begin to brown. Stir in garlic and cook until fragrant, about 1 minute. Add tomato paste, paprika, Worcestershire sauce, and soy sauce to mixture; stir until liquid evaporates. Stir in tomato juice, scraping any browned bits from pan, and cook until liquid is nearly gone. Take off heat and cool.

Whisk together chicken stock and egg. Sprinkle gelatin over mixture and fold in. Let sit 5 minutes.

In a large mixing bowl, break up meat into pieces. Pour cooled vegetable mixture into bowl and combine. Sprinkle crushed saltines over meat mixture. Add stock-egg mixture, salt, and mustard. Knead until all the elements are thoroughly combined. The meatloaf will be sticky.

Using a baking sheet that has a fitted rack, cover both sheet and rack with foil. Puncture foil on rack multiple times to let liquids pass through. Form meat mixture into three loaves, each about 8 inches long and 4 inches wide. Press a groove down the top center of each, allowing loaf to flatten slightly. Place in oven and cook for 1 hour or until thermometer reads 150°.

While meatloaf cooks, prepare glaze. Add all ingredients to a small saucepan and cook over medium heat until glaze reduces to 3/4 cup and thickens, about 15 minutes.

When meatloaf reaches 150°, change oven from bake to broil. Coat loaves with glaze and broil until bubbling, then add a second coating. Watch carefully that glaze doesn't burn. When coating caramelizes, remove from oven. Let loaves rest for 10 minutes and serve.

THIS IS THE ULTIMATE MEATLOAF RECIPE because it combines the tenderness of a traditional three-meat loaf with the beefiness of only using chuck. The secret is adding a mixture of egg, gelatin, and chicken stock to allow the meatloaf mixture to retain moisture.

The process of making the loaf seems like it has a lot of steps, but really, it has four components, each of which is separate and simple. The final stage of mixing it all together is best accomplished with your hands. If you are squeamish about diving in bare-handed, a supply of inexpensive plastic gloves will give you the protection you need to, well, knead.

This is one meatloaf that is as good cold as it is hot, and it slices nicely for sandwiches.

THIS MEATLOAF RECIPE CAN ALSO MAKE GREAT MEATBALLS WITH A FEW SMALL CHANGES. Add 2 teaspoons of Italian seasoning to the mixture and reduce the stock to 1/4 cup and the gelatin to 1/4 packet. You don't need to make a glaze.

Roll meat into 2-inch balls and place on foil-covered rack and cook for 20 minutes at 400°. Use the Simple Marinara sauce on page 13 over some spaghetti and meatballs, or put meatballs in a hoagie roll, cover with sauce and mozzarella, and toast in oven broiler until cheese melts.

TRADITIONAL HANUKKAH POTATO PANCAKES CAN VARY IN ALL KINDS OF WAYS—from the size of each one to the coarseness of the potato shred.

THESE LATKES ARE MEANT TO BE CRUNCHY AND AIRY, NOT LIKE A POTATO CAKE. They should be shredded with the coarsest shredder disk of a food processor or the largest holes in a manual shredder. When they are ready to fry, they are laid gently into the oil, a large spoonful at a time, and pressed flat to form a lacy pattern of loosely intertwined shreds, allowing oil to cook them all around.

Many recipes direct you to get rid of the extra starch by soaking the potatoes in warm water first, but that isn't necessary; what matters much more is extracting as much water as possible from the shredded potatoes, and paper towels just won't work. Using a tea towel like a screw press—twisting the top so liquid is forced out of the cloth—is the easiest way. You might even need two towels to get the liquid out.

TO VEER OFF THE TRADITIONAL PATH, try adding 1/2 cup Parmesan cheese to the batter for a nuttier taste, or add some shredded sweet potato to the mix for a sweeter latke. Traditional accompaniments are sour cream and apple sauce, but there are some interesting alternatives. Go Chinese with orange sauce, or try the plum sauce usually served with Peking duck.

Super Crispy Latkes

MAKES 24 FOUR-INCH LATKES

- **5 lbs** Russet potatoes (about 10 orange-sized)
- **1** large onion, chopped to small dice
- **2** eggs
- **3 Tbs** flour
- **2 tsp** salt
- **1/2 tsp** baking powder (optional)
- **3** scallions, green tops (optional)
- **2 cups** vegetable oil for frying

Peel potatoes and grate using the largest holes of a grater. Line a bowl with a clean kitchen tea towel draped over the rim and add potatoes. Wrap the potatoes in the tea towel and squeeze out as much moisture as you can. (You may need to use a second towel—there might be more than a cup of liquid.) Discard liquid and put potatoes back in bowl.

Add the diced onion, and sprinkle flour, salt, and baking powder (it's optional, so don't worry if you don't have any) over the potatoes. Beat the eggs until blended and add to the mixture. Stir to thoroughly integrate all the elements. Let sit for 15 minutes, stirring once or twice. Chop the scallions into 1/4-inch pieces, discarding white bottoms. Add to the mixture just before cooking and stir thoroughly.

In a 12-inch nonstick frying pan, pour oil to a depth of 1 inch. Heat until oil reaches 350°. Add a heaping serving spoon of potato mixture, and press flat into the oil with back of spoon. Each latke should be about 4 inches in diameter. Cook no more than 6 at a time in the pan. The latkes will bubble vigorously. Leave them alone to cook, but after a minute or so, shake the pan gently to ensure they aren't sticking.

When latkes are brown on the edges, about 2 minutes, turn them over using a spatula and a fork. After another minute or so, the latkes will be golden brown. Move them to a baking tray lined with paper towels to drain. Put the tray in a 200° oven to keep warm until ready to serve.

Serve with applesauce and sour cream.

Pan-Roasted Salmon with Hash

SERVES 6

FISH

- **2 lbs** salmon, skinned, with any pin bones removed
- **1** large shallot, diced fine
- **2 Tbs** soy sauce
- **2 Tbs** fish sauce
- **1/8 tsp** sugar
- **1/2 tsp** cornstarch
- **3 Tbs** olive oil
- **2 Tbs** lemon juice
- **1/4 cup** white wine

HASH

- **1 Tbs** olive oil
- **2 Tbs** butter
- **1 Tbs** fresh thyme
- **1 Tbs** fresh tarragon
- **1 Tbs** salt
- **2 slices** thick-cut bacon, cut into 1/4-inch dice
- **1 cup** Brussels sprouts, cut into quarters
- **1 cup** cauliflower and/or broccoli, broken into small florets
- **1** Spanish or sweet onion, cut pole-to-pole into 1/2-inch pieces
- **3** carrots, cut into 1/2-inch pieces
- **1** large zucchini, cut to 1/2-inch dice
- **1/2** fennel bulb, cut like onion
- **6** garlic cloves, sliced coarsely

Preheat oven to 400°. Start with a salmon fillet cut from the front of the fish. Cut into 6 thick pieces. Combine shallot, soy sauce, and fish sauce into a medium bowl with salmon. Marinate for 1/2 hour, turning fish once.

While the fish is marinating, prepare the hash. Heat a 12-inch oven-safe skillet over medium-high flame. Add chopped bacon and cook until browned, about 5 minutes, stirring occasionally. Remove bacon with a slotted spoon and reserve. Add oil and butter to the pan. Add spices and allow to bloom for 30 seconds. When foaming subsides, add garlic and onion and sauté until fragrant, about 1 minute. Add remaining vegetables. They will fill up the pan. Lower flame to medium heat; add salt and cook for 10 minutes, turning over the contents until vegetables show some browning. Transfer the vegetables to a rimmed baking sheet and arrange close together in one layer. Add reserved bacon. Cook in oven for 15 minutes.

Remove salmon from marinade and pat dry. Reserve marinade. Combine cornstarch and sugar and sprinkle lightly over salmon to cover. Add olive oil to the skillet you cooked the hash in, and heat until shimmering. Add salmon pieces to pan. Cook until well-browned on one side, about 4 minutes. Turn salmon over, cook for 1 minute more, and take off heat. Put skillet in oven and cook for 4 minutes or until fish is just opaque in the center.

Remove hash and salmon from oven, taking care not to burn yourself on the skillet handle. Reserve salmon on a plate. Add marinade to skillet and cook on stovetop 1 minute, scraping any brown bits from bottom. Add wine to pan and cook another minute. Toss hash in skillet to coat with marinade-wine mixture.

Serve hash in large, shallow bowl or high-sided plate, arranging salmon on top and spooning a teaspoon of lemon juice over each piece of fish.

PAN ROASTING FISH IS EASIER THAN IT SOUNDS. Quickly seared fish is finished in the oven at high heat. To ensure a good browning, cornstarch and sugar (not enough to taste sweet) lightly coat the salmon.

A single skillet does most of the work here—first to sauté the hash; then to cook the salmon; and finally, using the marinade plus a little white wine to make a sauce for tossing the hash in before serving.

THE HASH CAN BE THE CENTER OF ANOTHER MEAL WITHOUT THE SALMON. Cut a spaghetti squash in half lengthwise, scrape out seeds, and boil in salted water for 15 minutes. Scrape flesh with a fork to form the distinctive strands, combine with hash and 2 cups of the Simple Marinara sauce on page 13, plus 1/2 cup grated Parmesan cheese. Put the mixture back into the squash halves and cover with a slice of fresh mozzarella cheese. Put into oven and cook for 15 minutes until cheese is bubbling and starting to brown on top. Generously serves two.

JEWISH MOTHERS NEVER SEEM TO USE RECIPES, THEY JUST "KNOW" HOW TO MAKE THINGS. Chopped liver is the classic European Jewish appetizer, often served with challah or lettuce and tomato. It shares a lot with French pâté, but probably wouldn't be caught dead in a bistro, preferring to reside in a deli in Queens.

The combination of the cooked egg and the chopped liver transforms the texture, color, and taste of the dish in unexpected ways, effectively cutting the "liver-y" taste and changing the consistency. Many people who don't like offal *do* like chopped liver, perhaps because it is so far removed from the original texture and shape, and perhaps because it's a perfectly savory snack that brings back warm memories of holidays past.

Of course, my *bubbe* made this recipe in an ancient wooden bowl, chopping the liver and eggs with a *mezzaluna,* the traditional crescent-shaped blade in the picture. With the help of a food processor, the whole dish can be made in a half hour.

My mother claims—with pride—that she never measures anything. She "just knows" when she has added the right amount in any recipe, whether it was this chopped liver or *lokshun kugel* (noodle casserole) or any of the other things she learned to make from *her* mother. However, getting this recipe right required some actual measuring—which was done behind her back.

Mom's Chopped Liver

SERVES 8-12 AS AN APPETIZER

1 lb chicken livers
4 eggs, hard-boiled, room temperature
4 Tbs schmaltz (rendered chicken fat) or clarified butter
1 medium onion, diced fine
2 Tbs sherry
10 peppercorns, coarsely crushed
1/2 Tbs salt

Bring salted water in a 4-quart saucepan to a boil. Clean livers, pulling off fatty membranes. Add livers to the boiling water and turn heat down to medium. Cook for 5 minutes; and immediately drain. Livers should still be slightly pink in the middle. Be careful not to overcook the livers, or the final result will be dry.

In a 10-inch skillet, melt schmaltz or butter; add crushed pepper and cook for 1 minute to allow the pepper to bloom. Add onion and lower heat to medium. Cook onion until very soft but not browned. Stir in sherry, then add livers and toss, sautéing for 1 minute. Take off heat and cool.

In a food processor, add peeled hardboiled eggs, reserving 1 yolk. Pulse eggs two to three times for a few seconds until they are finely chopped but not puréed. Using a rubber spatula, scrape eggs into a deep 3-quart mixing bowl.

Add liver mixture to processor. Pulse for 5-second intervals until the mixture is puréed, about 20 seconds total. Using a rubber spatula, scrape liver out of processor bowl into the mixing bowl containing the chopped egg, and gently fold until completely combined. The liver-and-egg mixture is transformed into a mocha-colored, somewhat coarse paté.

Spread the mixture onto a 10-inch plate or tart pan. Crumble reserved yolk over the liver for garnish and refrigerate for 1 hour.

Serve a portion on a leaf of Romaine, with sweet gherkins, pickled pearl onions, and challah toast points.

Cashew Shrimp Stir Fry

SERVES 6

- **2 cups** cooked, cooled white rice
- **2 lbs** shrimp (about 24 extra large), shelled and deveined
- **3 oz** cashews, unsalted
- **1** large red bell pepper, sliced into large julienne
- **1** stalk celery, cut into 1/8-inch slices
- **1 cup** broccoli florets
- **6** garlic cloves, minced
- **1** large sweet onion, cut into 1/2-inch slices pole-to-pole
- **6** scallions, cut into 2-inch pieces
- **1** jalapeño pepper, seeded and diced fine
- **2** eggs, lightly scrambled
- **1/4 cup** vegetable oil
- **1/2 tsp** cornstarch
- **1 oz** fresh ginger, peeled and cut into thin strips
- **1/4 cup** soy sauce
- **2 Tbs** fish sauce
- **2 Tbs** sugar
- **2 Tbs** rice vinegar
- **2 Tbs** fresh lime juice

Prepare shrimp and each vegetable in a separate bowl, ready for adding to the dish. Mix soy sauce, fish sauce, sugar, vinegar, and lime juice together, and hold for the end.

Preheat large skillet or wok until very hot. A drop of water should skitter across the bottom. Add 2 tablespoons oil and heat until smoking. Add onion, pepper, and celery to pan. Sauté until onion is browned on edges and celery and pepper are softened, about 2 minutes. Add garlic and cook until fragrant, about 1 minute. Remove from heat and reserve in large bowl.

Add another tablespoon oil, allow to heat. Sprinkle cornstarch on shrimp and toss to lightly cover, then add to pan. Shrimp will cook quickly. Keep turning the shrimp until they are nearly cooked in the center, about 1-2 minutes. Remove from pan and add to bowl of reserved vegetables.

Add remaining oil, allow to heat. Pour in eggs; add jalapeño and scallions and quickly scramble together. Add ginger and cashews and cook until cashews are fragrant and browning. Add rice and quickly toss until beginning to brown, about 4 minutes.

Add reserved ingredients from bowl, including any juices, and continue to sauté together. Add sauce mixture and continue stirring to combine, scraping any *fond* on the bottom of the pan dissolved by the sauce, until rice is a golden brown and shrimp are just cooked through, another 3 minutes.

Serve immediately.

A STIR FRY IS ALL ABOUT PREP. The cooking itself should happen inside of 15 minutes and, in this recipe, is done in a series of stages to keep the oil and the pan hot. The aromatics go in first, then the protein, which could just as easily be cubed chicken or beef. It is easy to overcook shrimp, so after the shrimp turn white and orange in the pan, but are still a little raw in the center, remove them. The last few minutes of stir-frying will finish them.

The sauce has tons of glutamates to add savoriness to the dish. Soy and fish sauces are high in the fifth taste, *umami,* which literally means “delicious taste” in Japanese but has been adapted as “savory” in English.

SOMETHING MAGICAL HAPPENS WHEN STARCHY ARBORIO RICE IS COOKED. The release of starch from slow stirring beautifully complements the soft grains; however, many people aren't thrilled about spending 20 minutes stirring rice. My technique adds half of the stock all at once and requires only a bit of attention until the last 5 minutes of the process.

THERE IS ONLY ONE THING TO WATCH FOR IN MAKING RISOTTO—HITTING THE EXACT MOMENT WHEN THE COOKING SHOULD END. Too little and you have chalky rice; too much and it's a gummy mess. My cooking method takes some of the guesswork out of the process, but there's no substitute for tasting as it nears completion. The secret is knowing that the final bit of cooking happens as you add the last liquids and cheese. If you begin that process when the rice is just a bit underdone—edible but not tasty—the final result will be perfect.

THE CHEESE MAKES A BIG DIFFERENCE IN THE QUALITY OF THE DISH. This recipe uses half of what many suggest, so get the highest quality Parmesan you can. The best stuff is aged 18 months, and comes from the Parmigiano-Reggiano region of Italy. Fresh grating with a microplane grater creates the perfect shred.

THIS RECIPE CAN BE THE START OF MANY RISOTTO VARIATIONS. You can use sautéed mushrooms, diced pancetta and peas, julienned peppers and snow peas, even tiny meatballs and marinara sauce. The risotto is a rich accompaniment for lamb and chicken and works well with spicy braised dishes.

Risotto with Lemon and Asparagus

SERVES 4 AS A MAIN COURSE / 8 AS A SIDE DISH

1 Tbs butter
3 Tbs olive oil
1 cup arborio rice
8 cups chicken stock
1 cup dry white wine
1/2 lb asparagus (about 16 thin stalks)
1/2 Parmigiano-Reggiano cheese, freshly grated
3 Tbs parsley, chopped
3 Tbs lemon zest (about 1 lemon), cut in thin strips
1/4 cup lemon juice, freshly squeezed
1 tsp salt

Heat chicken stock in microwave in 8-cup measuring cup until very hot.

Trim woody bottom from asparagus and rinse. Place on dampened paper towels. Roll towels around asparagus and place in microwave. Cook on high for 2 minutes. Place asparagus immediately in cold water. When cool, cut off tips and cut stems into 1/2-inch chunks. Set aside.

In an 8-quart saucepan, heat olive oil and butter over medium-high heat until foaming subsides; add rice. Sauté rice in oil-butter for 2 minutes until rice shows a distinct "eye" in the center of each grain and becomes fragrant. Reduce heat to low; add wine and stir until liquid is nearly absorbed. Add salt, 4 cups of the stock all at once, and stir to incorporate.

Cover and cook over very low heat for 15 minutes, stirring once or twice. Liquid should not be completely absorbed. Begin adding stock to the rice 1/2 cup at a time, stirring slowly to incorporate. Rice will become creamy. Keep adding stock until rice is just slightly less than *al dente*. You will probably not use all 8 cups of stock.

Add lemon juice and lemon peel and cook another 2 minutes until juice is absorbed and rice is done. Add cheese and stir gently to incorporate. Add asparagus pieces and parsley. Toss and serve immediately.

Shrimp and Grits

SERVES 6

- **9 Tbs** Quaker grits (NOT quick or instant varieties)
- **1 tsp** salt
- **3½ cups** 2% milk (or 1½ cup whole milk and 2 cups water)
- **3 Tbs** butter
- **1/4 cup** whole milk or half-and-half
- **1/2 cup** Parmesan, grated
- **2 lbs** extra-large shrimp (about 24), peeled and deveined, tail-on
- **2** slices thick bacon, diced
- **1** red bell pepper, diced
- **1** medium onion, diced
- **6** garlic cloves, minced
- **2 Tbs** Worcestershire sauce
- **1 Tbs** balsamic vinegar
- **1/2 tsp** paprika
- **1/2 tsp** chile powder
- **1/2 tsp** salt
- **6** spring onions, cut into 1/2-inch pieces, discarding tips
- **12 oz** tomato juice
- **1 tsp** hot sauce (or to taste)
- **12** eggs, poached (optional)

Grits

Add grits, salt and milk to a deep 3-quart microwavable ceramic bowl and stir to combine. Cover tightly with plastic wrap and place bowl on top of a paper towel in microwave. Cook on medium high ("8" in a 1500-watt unit) for 12 minutes, checking occasionally. The grits should be soft, cooked to the consistency of cream of wheat.

The bowl will be very hot. The grits should be done. If not, add more water as needed and continue for another 4 minutes, stirring and replacing plastic wrap. When done, add butter, 1 tablespoon at a time. Add whole milk or half-and-half to thin the grits as needed until they are thick but stir easily. Add cheese and stir to combine. Cover and set aside. Add more milk if the mixture becomes too thick—it should be thick but not set.

Poach eggs, if using, and reserve in warm water.

Shrimp

Place diced bacon in a 12-inch nonstick skillet at medium heat. Cook bacon until crisp and fat is rendered. Remove bacon and set aside. Turn heat to high. Add shrimp and sauté quickly until just cooked through, about 2 minutes. Remove and set aside.

Lower heat to medium. Add pepper and onion and sauté until softened. Add garlic and cook until fragrant, about 1 minute. Add balsamic vinegar and Worcestershire sauce. Sprinkle in paprika, chile powder and salt. Stir and cook until liquid just evaporates. Add spring onion pieces and cook until they wilt, about 30 seconds. Add tomato juice, stirring to deglaze pan. Add hot sauce to taste; return bacon and shrimp to pan and combine. Cook for 1-2 minutes more.

Place a heaping serving of grits in the center of a large, shallow bowl or rimmed plate, pressing down to make two depressions. Add poached eggs to depressions; then add shrimp and sauce around grits and serve.

HERE IS A DISH THAT IS JUST AS GOOD AT DINNER AS IT IS AT BREAKFAST. The creamy cheese grits are a great contrast to the garlicky, spicy sauce the shrimp are tossed in.

It's easy to make **Quaker** grits in the microwave, but for an extra special treat, use **Anson Mills Quick Grits**. These require longer cooking than Quaker grits. They're made with heirloom corn in artisanal batches and taste surprisingly of fresh corn, but the more widely available **Bob's Red Mill Corn Grits** are also very nice.

THESE GRITS COOK BETTER ON THE STOVETOP. Once the grits start bubbling, turn the heat as low as you can. The grits need more stirring and have to be watched carefully—a small lapse of attention, and they can easily burn. They usually take twice as long as Quaker grits, too because they are ground into bigger pieces—but they are well worth the extra time and attention.

***ONGLET* IS A FRENCH TERM FOR HANGER STEAK**, a less-well-known cut that is sometimes referred to as the "butcher's cut." It's a flavorful but sometimes chewy piece of meat that sits between the two loins, so there's only one per steer. The piece is usually butchered to cut away a large tendon that runs asymmetrically along the length of the cut. It yields a 1- to 2-lb steak about 10 inches long and 3 inches thick on the large side and a smaller steak just as long but only about 1½ inches thick. Buy the larger side for this dish.

This recipe cooks the meat in a low oven and then sears the surface quickly in a hot skillet so the meat is done no more than medium rare. Of course, grilling the *onglet* over a hot fire is a tasty alternative. Prepare by cutting 1/2-inch round medallions perpendicular to the length, but sliced at an angle.

The salad provides a crisp and citrus-y contrast to the rich meat. The dressing is loosely based on one that used to be served at a crêperie chain called the Magic Pan, as part of a romaine salad with mandarin oranges and almonds. Although the Magic Pan is long out of business, a quick online search reveals many entries for the recipe—a testament to the power of flavor and memory.

Onglet Salad

SERVES 4

MEAT

2 lbs hanger steak
1 Tbs kosher salt
ground black pepper to taste
1 Tbs oil

SALAD

3 cups romaine, hand-shredded
1 cup frisee and radicchio
1/2 cup feta cheese, crumbled
1/2 purple onion, cut into thin rings
20 cherry tomatoes, cut in half
20 orange segments, membranes removed

DRESSING

1 cup olive oil
2 Tbs sugar
1/4 tsp salt
1 Tbs mayonnaise
1 tsp fresh tarragon
1 tsp dry mustard
1 Tbs fresh lemon juice
1/4 cup orange juice
1 clove garlic, lightly crushed

Set oven to 300°. The hanger steak will be in one or two long pieces. Salt and pepper the steaks generously. Place meat in the oven and roast gently until a quick-reading thermometer reads 110°, about 15 minutes. On the stove, heat a 10-inch skillet until very hot; add oil. Sear hanger steak on all sides, continuing until well-browned, about 5 minutes. The interior should be 130°. Cover loosely and let rest.

Combine all salad ingredients except tomatoes and oranges. Make dressing by adding all the ingredients to a small jar and shaking vigorously until emulsified. The dressing should be a nice yellow-orange color. Add 3/4 cup dressing to salad and toss to coat.

Cut hanger steak perpendicular to length at slight angle to make small medallions. Divide salad among four bowls, place tomatoes and orange segments on top. Finally, splay steak on top of salad and serve. Bring reserved dressing to table.

Decadent Smashed Potatoes

SERVES 6

- **8** Yukon Gold potatoes, the size of tennis balls
- **10** garlic cloves, peeled
- **1** large sweet onion, cut in half and then into 1-inch slices, pole-to-pole
- **1/3 cup** olive oil
- **1 tsp** salt
- **1 tsp** fresh rosemary, chopped
- **1/2 tsp** paprika

In an 8-quart pot, boil potatoes in salted water until almost done, about 20 minutes. Do not peel or cut them. During the last 5 minutes of cooking, add peeled garlic cloves. Remove from heat when you can pierce with a fork (but the potato doesn't fall apart). Drain potatoes and pat dry with paper towels. Score the potatoes all over with a knife to break their skins.

Add half the oil to a cold, nonstick, 10-inch sauté pan (with straight sides) and then add the potatoes, distributing them in one layer in the pan. Using a meat pounder or potato masher, press potatoes to smash them, breaking open skin and pressing them to about half their original height. Wedge onions and garlic amid the potatoes and sprinkle salt and rosemary on top.

Put pan on medium heat and pour the rest of the oil evenly around food between pieces, shaking pan to distribute the oil. Cook gently over medium heat without disturbing contents for 20 minutes. Shake pan to make sure potatoes aren't sticking, and cook another 10 minutes. Potatoes should be browning on the bottom and should release from the pan with a gentle shake. Working in sections, turn over potatoes, trying to keep them from crumbling, if possible. Continue to cook the other side another 15 to 30 minutes until the oil is absorbed, the potatoes are golden brown and crispy, the garlic is very soft, and the onions are soft and browned. Sprinkle paprika over top. Serve immediately, directly from the pan.

IMAGINE THE CRISPINESS OF FRENCH FRIES, the creaminess of baked potatoes, and the savory aromatics of hash browns all cooked up in one pan—that's what these potatoes are like. They are a bit too much for every day, but, paired with rich meat like a thick steak or short ribs, they are addictive.

THE TRICK HERE IS PATIENCE. The potatoes need to fry gently, and any attempt to disturb them will make them fall apart. After all, the potatoes are already almost completely cooked. The pan-frying finishes the interiors while crisping the exteriors and combining the flavors of the aromatics and spices.

LET POTATOES COOK FOR 20 MINUTES BEFORE BEGINNING TO CHECK THE UNDERSIDES. When they are ready to turn, they will release from the pan. If they are getting too brown, the pan is too hot. Reduce to medium after turning and allow to cook through.

Keep the potatoes crisp and warm in a 250° oven, because people *will* want seconds. For even more decadence, serve with a dollop of sour cream.

YUKON GOLD POTATOES ARE ALMOST REQUIRED FOR THIS DISH. Potato varieties are different in their starch and moisture content. Waxier potatoes are better in stews and soups, and starchier potatoes make better baking potatoes and fries. The Yukon Gold is somewhere in the middle. A Russet in this dish will fall apart, and a Red Bliss will be gummy.

THERE IS ANOTHER CHOICE, THOUGH—FINGERLING POTATOES. Using these smaller, thumb-sized potatoes makes this dish much flatter, and a bit more elegant. Yellow fingerlings work well, but if you find a bag of mixed yellow, red, and purple fingerlings, the final dish is even more colorful. Reduce the oil to 1/4 cup.

ONE MORE COOKING OPTION makes the dish even easier to produce, since it eliminates turning the potatoes. Follow the recipe, but add *all* the oil by pouring it over the potatoes once they are smashed in the pan, instead of adding part on the bottom. Shake to distribute and then place the pan in a 400° oven and cook for 30 minutes. The spuds comes out pretty crispy, but not as evenly browned.

SOMETIMES THE SIDES CAN MAKE A MEAL. The ones on the next two spreads are easy to prepare, require very little effort to cook, and taste surprisingly complex.

The Brussels sprouts recipe will convert people who think they don't like the vegetable. The orange juice reduces to a sweet syrup, and the pistachios add crunch. It's also amazing what OJ and maple syrup can do for sweet potatoes—but it's the balsamic that makes the difference in both recipes.

Slow roasting can turn onions and tomatoes into wondrously tasty things, as the starches are converted to sugars and the outsides caramelize.

The rice is actually a pilaf—and not *that* super buttery, but calling it that did convince my kids to eat it. The corn sauté looks awesome if you use bi-color corn or mix white and yellow sweet corn. The secret is to cook it as little as possible, especially if it's summer and the corn is local.

And what dinner wouldn't be enhanced by some great bread? These breadsticks were a highlight at Four & Twenty Blackbirds, a restaurant in Flint Hill, Virginia. They are easy to make and freeze really well, so make a double batch.

Brussels Sprouts for Haters

SERVES 6

2 cups	Brussels sprouts, cut into 1/4-inch slices, vertically
2 Tbs	olive oil
3	garlic cloves, sliced thin
2	shallots, diced fine
3/4 cup	orange juice
1 Tbs	Champagne vinegar
1/4 cup	shelled pistachio nuts

Add olive oil to 10-inch sauté pan over high heat until shimmering. Add shallots and cook until soft, about 2 minutes. Add garlic, stir together and cook until fragrant, about 1 minute. Lower heat to medium, add Brussels sprouts; and cook until sprouts begin to brown, about 5 minutes. Add orange juice and vinegar; stir with wooden spoon to deglaze pan. Cover and cook until sprouts are tender and juice has reduced to a syrup, around 8 minutes. Add pistachios and stir to combine.

Simplest Sweet Potatoes

SERVES 6

4	sweet potatoes
3 Tbs	butter
3 Tbs	maple syrup
1/2 cup	orange juice
1/4 tsp	ground ginger
1/4 tsp	salt
1 Tbs	balsamic vinegar

Preheat oven to 400°. Place sweet potatoes on baking sheet and roast 45 minutes or until very soft. Remove from oven and allow to cool 10 minutes. Remove skins and place flesh in a large bowl. Add all the other ingredients and whip with a fork until well combined and fluffy.

Roasted Sweet Onions

SERVES 6

3	large Vidalia or Texas Sweet onions
2 Tbs	olive oil
1 cup	chicken stock
2 tsp	fresh rosemary, chopped
3 Tbs	bread crumbs
1/4 tsp	kosher salt

Preheat oven to 400°. Peel outer skin from onions, and carefully trim top and root, leaving as much as possible. Cut onion into quarters lengthwise, leaving part of the dense section near the roots on each piece.

Place onions close together in a 2-quart baking dish, rounded outsides down and squared-off cuts pointing up. Pour stock over onions and then drizzle with oil. Sprinkle onions with rosemary and salt and place in oven. Roast for 40 minutes, basting occasionally. When the onion segments begin to separate and brown, sprinkle bread crumbs over them. Continue baking another 15 minutes until crumbs are brown. Remove from oven and allow to rest for 10 minutes before serving.

Super-Buttery Rice

SERVES 6

- **1 cup** long-grain white rice
- **1** small shallot, minced
- **3 Tbs** butter
- **2¼ cups** chicken stock
- **1 tsp** salt
- **1/4 cup** chopped parsley
- **2 Tbs** lemon juice
- **1/4 cup** almond slivers

Rinse rice in a strainer under cold water until the water runs clear. Shake rice dry. In a 2-quart pot over medium-high heat, melt butter until it foams. Add shallot and cook until softened, about 1 minute. Add rice and almonds; sauté until rice becomes fragrantly nutty, about 2 minutes. Add stock and reduce heat to low simmer. Cover, using a tea towel between pot and top to absorb steam. Cook for 20 minutes. Add chopped parsley and let sit another 10 minutes. Add lemon juice and stir to fluff.

Slow-Roasted Tomatoes

SERVES 6

- **24** Roma tomatoes
- **10** fresh basil leaves, coarsely chopped
- **3 Tbs** olive oil
- **1/4 Tbs** dried lemon peel
- **1/4 Tbs** kosher salt
- **1/4 Tbs** oregano
- **1/4 cup** Parmesan (optional)

Heat oven to 225°. Remove stem from each tomato and, using a paring knife, carve a small "X" into the skin at the stem dimple. In a bowl, toss tomatoes in olive oil to coat and place in a baking dish so they are tightly packed. Scrape remaining oil from bowl over tomatoes. Sprinkle basil, salt, oregano, and lemon peel over tomatoes and place in oven. Lightly cover with foil. Bake in oven for 1½ to 2 hours. Tomatoes will render liquid. Remove foil, sprinkle cheese (if using) lightly and evenly over tomatoes, and cook for another 15 minutes until cheese has melted and is lightly browned.

Fresh Corn Sauté

SERVES 6

- **4** ears sweet corn
- **3 Tbs** butter
- **1** medium onion, diced
- **1/2** red bell pepper, diced
- **1 tsp** sugar
- **1 tsp** salt
- **1/8 tsp** cayenne pepper
- **3 Tbs** crème fraîche or sour cream
- **1 tsp** lime juice
- **1 tsp** fresh parsley, chopped

Cut kernels from cobs and use fork to separate. In a 10-inch skillet, melt butter until foaming subsides and then add onion and pepper. Cook until softened. Add kernels and sprinkle with cayenne. Continue sautéing, stirring to combine until kernels are cooked through but still a bit crunchy, about 3–4 minutes, depending on the freshness of the corn. Remove from heat, stir in parsley, crème fraîche, and lime juice.

Four & Twenty Breadsticks

24 PIECES

- **7–8** cups of flour
- **5 tsp** yeast in 2 cups hot water
- **2 Tbs** olive oil
- **2 Tbs** vegetable oil
- **1** medium onion, finely chopped
- **1** stalk celery, finely chopped
- **1 tsp** fennel seed, chopped
- **1 tsp** thyme
- **1 tsp** fresh ground pepper
- **2 tsp** salt

Heat oil to shimmering in 10-inch sauté pan. Add onion and cook until transparent, but not soft. Add celery and fennel seed and continue to cook until celery softens.

Dissolve yeast in hot water. Using a stand mixer, add onion and celery mixture, salt and pepper, thyme, and olive oil; pour in yeast and water. With mixer at low speed, gradually add flour until dough comes together and pulls away from side of bowl, about 2–3 minutes.

Remove the still-sticky dough from the bowl and roll out on floured surface. Knead by hand until dough is resilient. Divide dough in half, placing each half on a greased baking sheet. Rub olive oil over dough; cover with wax paper and a damp towel. Let dough rise in a warm place for 20 minutes.

Heat oven to 350°. Form dough into 8-inch breadsticks no thicker than your thumb, curling one end like a crook. Bake 20 minutes until lightly browned.

THERE IS NO AVOIDING THE MULTI-STEP APPROACH THAT IS PART OF MAKING A CHICKEN POT PIE. It's always better to cook the vegetables and chicken separately, and then combine everything at the end. This recipe makes it as close to a one-pot dish as possible. By poaching the chicken and cooking the vegetables at the same time in stock, the stock for the *béchamel* is also being enhanced. Using the same pot to make the *roux* and the sauce saves a cleanup—and gets the last bits of flavor out of the pot.

The basic pie crust depends on two important factors: using cold butter and then letting the crust get cold again in the refrigerator. Floating the crust over the filling in a round baking dish requires a cold crust, or else the dough will begin to dissolve before it cooks. Adding some dried herbs gives the crust more savoriness. And the vodka makes the crust more tender by inhibiting the formation of gluten. Any cheap vodka will do, and it leaves no trace.

THESE PIES ARE ALSO GREAT MADE IN 18-OUNCE RAMEKINS, SO EVERYONE GETS THEIR OWN POT PIE. The crust recipe will make only enough crust for four individual pies, so double the crust ingredients to make enough for six.

Savory Pie Crust

ONE 12-INCH CRUST

1 1/4 cups	all-purpose flour
1/4 tsp	thyme
1/4 tsp	sage
1/4 tsp	salt
1/2 cup	butter, chilled and diced
4 Tbs	ice water
4 Tbs	cold vodka

In a large bowl, combine flour, spices, and salt. Cut in butter until mixture resembles coarse crumbs. Mix water and vodka together and add—a tablespoon at a time—just until mixture forms a ball. Wrap in plastic and refrigerate for at least 4 hours or overnight.

Roll dough out to a 12-inch diameter for a round 10-inch baking dish (or 2 inches wider than dish being used). Fold dough in half and then in half again for easy handling later, and keep refrigerated until needed.

Chicken Pot Pie

SERVES 6

4	skinless, boneless chicken breasts
3 cups	chicken stock
1 cup	half-and-half
3	carrots, cut into 1/2-inch dice
3	Yukon Gold potatoes, peeled and cut into 1/2-inch dice
1	medium onion, cut into 1-inch pieces
1 Tbs	fresh tarragon, chopped
3 Tbs	flour
3 Tbs	butter
1	bay leaf
1 tsp	salt
1/4 tsp	fresh ground pepper
1 cup	frozen peas
1	12-inch Savory Pie Crust

In a 6-quart Dutch oven, poach chicken breasts in stock, along with tarragon, onions, garlic, carrots and potatoes, about 20 minutes. Strain stock to measuring cup and reserve. Remove vegetables and reserve separately. Cut poached chicken into irregular 3/4-inch pieces and add to reserved vegetables.

Preheat oven to 375°. Wipe out pot and add butter. When foaming subsides, add flour and cook until lightly brown. Add half-and-half and whisk until mixture thickens. Add stock and bay leaf, and cook over medium heat until mixture thickens, about 10 minutes. Remove bay leaf. Add frozen peas and combine.

In a 3-quart, 10-inch round baking dish, combine sauce, chicken, and vegetables. Unfold and position crust over dish, allowing edges to drape. Roll up edges until crust sits inside dish. Use fork to scallop edges against inside edge of dish. Make several slits in crust to allow steam to escape. Place in oven and cook for 30 minutes or until crust is golden and pie bubbles.

Allow pot pie to rest for 10 minutes and serve.

Chicken Thigh Bake

SERVES 6

- **12** chicken thighs, skin-on and bone-in
- **1/2 cup** table salt
- **1/2 cup** sugar
- **1 Tbs** olive oil
- **3 cups** brown rice pilaf
- **2 Tbs** AURAS Spice Mix (page 9)

Mix a brine for the chicken thighs by combining 1/2 cup table salt and 1/2 cup sugar in 2 quarts water in a saucepan and heating until dissolved. Add ice cubes until brine cools to room temperature. Place thighs in a deep bowl and pour in brine. Let the mixture sit for at least 1 hour but not more than 3 hours.

Preheat oven to 400°. Remove thighs from brine, rinse and pat dry. In a 10-inch round baking dish, add rice, vegetables, and parsley and stir together. Take chicken thighs and mound around rice mixture, skin side out, to completely encase the mound. Brush thighs with olive oil, sprinkle spice mix over them. Place in center of oven. Cook uncovered for 1 hour, basting periodically with rendered juices. Chicken is done when meat reaches 170°.

Serve directly from baking dish.

Brown Rice Pilaf

SERVES 6

- **2 Tbs** olive oil
- **1** medium onion, diced
- **2** carrots, diced
- **1** stalk celery, diced
- **1 cup** brown rice
- **1 cup** chicken stock
- **1 cup** water
- **1 tsp** salt
- **1/4 cup** fresh flat-leaf parsley, chopped

Heat oil in a 3-quart pot and add onions, carrots and celery. Sauté for 1 minute and add rice. Continue cooking, stirring vegetables and rice until rice is slightly browned, about another 2 minutes.

Add stock, water, and salt and stir. When mixture boils, reduce to very low heat and cover. Cook without disturbing for 40 minutes. Check rice. Water should be absorbed and rice should be slightly chewy. If there is still water, cook another 5 minutes. Stir in parsley and use mixture in chicken thigh bake.

THIS IS A ONE-DISH BAKE THAT MAKES THE MOST OF THE FLAVOR IN CHICKEN THIGHS. Using them as a cover for the rice, which cooks like stuffing in a whole bird, helps the skins become crisp and the fats and juices saturate the rice, while the rice keeps the meat moist as it cooks.

DARK MEAT DOESN'T GET THE RESPECT IT DESERVES IN AMERICA, but it's the overwhelming preference in the rest of the world. It's no wonder. Properly cooked legs and thighs are meaty and much more flavorful than breast meat, and much less prone to drying out. Using bone-in and skin-on thighs is important in this recipe because it maximizes not just the flavor of the chicken but also the rice underneath. If you must, you can always take the skin off before you eat it.

The final dish looks pretty impressive, especially if you use an artistic ceramic baking dish.

De-Boned Herbed Turkey Breast

SERVES 8

ALTHOUGH IT SEEMS WEIRD TO WRAP SOMETHING IN PLASTIC AND PUT IT IN THE OVEN, professional chefs like to use a vacuum-packed, food-in-water-bath technique called *sous vide* to super-slow-cook meats and fish at really low temperatures. This technique is similar. These turkey breasts are stacked with an herb mixture between them, rolled securely in plastic wrap into a roll, covered with foil and then roasted in very low heat for several hours, ensuring they will stay moist.

This is really a lot easier than tying with string, and has a much better presentation in the end. Don't worry, the plastic wrap won't melt, and when the turkey emerges from its foil-and-plastic cocoon, it will have magically formed into a beautiful roll, which will have a pretty stripe of green herbs in the center when cut. All that remains is crisping the skin in a hot oven while making a gravy with the liquid that has collected during the slow roast.

This turkey roll makes an excellent cold entrée at a party, as it will slice paper thin once it has been refrigerated.

- **6–7 lb** fresh whole turkey breast
- **1/4 cup** table salt
- **1/4 cup** sugar
- **1/2 cup** fresh parsley, chopped
- **1/4 cup** fresh basil, chopped
- **2 Tbs** fresh thyme
- **1/4 cup** olive oil
- **1 Tbs** paprika
- **2 Tbs** butter

Rinse turkey breast and pat dry. Carefully remove the skin, starting at the thick folds in the back, loosening with your fingers. Pull the skin back from the breast toward the small end, keeping it in one piece as much as possible. Reserve skin.

Using a sharp boning knife, take breasts off the bone by inserting knife several inches at top of breast, feeling for the breastbone. Following along the bone, cut toward the small end. When the top part of the breast is cut away, follow down the side of the breast to the bottom and remove the entire breast from the bone. Repeat process on the other side. Place breasts on foil, side by side, with one thin end next to one thick end, and underside of breasts facing up. Mix salt and sugar together and apply liberally to breasts. Let sit for 30 minutes; then rinse off mixture and pat dry, returning breasts to the same position on foil.

In a blender or food processor, pulse together the parsley, basil, thyme, and olive oil to form a paste. Spread half the paste on the underside of the breasts, and liberally spread the rest on the exposed top parts as they rest on the foil.

Place one breast on top of the other so the thin and thick ends are opposite, forming a more uniform shape. Take the reserved skin, and, as best as possible, drape over the combined breasts and wrap around them, removing any small pieces and fatty parts. Make sure the seam between the breasts is completely covered.

Spread a 2-foot-long piece of plastic wrap on a clean surface. Move turkey so it sits horizontally at one end of plastic, and tightly wrap turkey in plastic so it forms a tight roll. Take a second sheet of plastic and wrap in the perpendicular direction, so turkey is completely sealed in plastic and is a compact cylindrical shape.

Using a fresh piece of heavy-duty foil, wrap plastic-wrapped turkey in foil and seal ends. Place turkey on rimmed baking sheet in a 180° (yes, 180°) oven. Use instant-read thermometer to test meat after 2 hours (carefully insert probe through foil and plastic at top) and continue to monitor until temperature reaches 140°—another hour or so, depending on the size of the breast and the actual oven temperature.

Remove from oven and increase temperature to 400°. Carefully unwrap turkey from foil and plastic and reserve liquid. Brush butter all over skin; sprinkle with paprika and return to oven, with any exposed meat on the bottom. Continue to roast until skin is golden and crisp and meat temperature is 160°, about 20 minutes. Remove from oven, cover loosely with foil and let sit for 15 minutes. Use reserved liquid to make a quick gravy and serve turkey sliced, with gravy.

Softest Egg Scramble

SERVES 4

8	eggs
2 Tbs	butter
1 tsp	shallot, minced
1 tsp	tarragon
1	spring onion, finely diced
1/2 tsp	salt (or to taste)
1/4 tsp	dry mustard
2 oz	heavy cream
dash	hot sauce (or to taste)

Crack eggs into mixing bowl and whisk vigorously into a uniform liquid. Add salt, tarragon, mustard, hot sauce and mix. In a 1-quart saucepan over low heat, melt butter and add shallot. Cook for 1 minute until shallot softens. Add spring onion; cook for 1 minute more. Turn off heat and wait 2 minutes for pan to cool. Using a simmer ring if needed (see note) and the lowest setting on your stove, add egg mixture and stir slowly to incorporate the aromatics. Let sit for 2 minutes and then stir occasionally, folding cooked egg from edges back into the middle. The egg mixture will gradually thicken in 8-10 minutes, depending on temperature. Before mixture completely congeals, it will be in a glossy, thick state like yogurt. Take off heat and stir in cream. Continue stirring off-burner, allowing residual heat in pan to finish the cooking, until the eggs are barely set and wobbly. Serve right away. The curds will be extremely tender, almost a custard.

ADDITIONS: At the last stages of making the eggs, where the recipe calls for cream, you can try adding different things instead. Crumbled goat cheese or Stilton, or cubes of cream cheese, make an excellent addition to these eggs. You could also add diced avocado and a tablespoon of salsa at the end.

Another approach is to begin the egg recipe with crumbled sausage cooked slowly before adding the aromatics. Although this won't create as smooth a curd, it is very savory.

THE DRY AND CLUMPY CURDS of diner-style scrambled eggs are from another planet compared to these delicate, custardy eggs. Yes, they take more attention and thrice the time to cook, but the results are worth it. They pair well with sausage and bacon.

These eggs are much denser than regular scrambled eggs, so don't be surprised if they take up a lot less space on the plate. But that's part of the charm.

This recipe actually works best in a double boiler, where the bottom of the top pot is suspended above steaming water. But low, low flame and a bit more attention work almost as well, and with less fuss. You may need a simmer ring, though, if your lowest simmer setting is still too hot. A simmer ring sits on the burner, elevating your pot several inches above the heat. In a pinch, you can make one out of aluminum foil, rolling a large piece into a ring.

The Best Bacon and Sausage

Supermarket bacon is fine, but specialty brands that can be delivered to your door will blow away the typical Oscar Mayer strip.

From Chicago, **Nueske's** bacon has a deep applewood smoking. **Benton's** bacon, from Nashville, truly deserves to be called a breakfast meat—these thick, intensely hickory-smoked salty strips of pig heaven are best cooked low and slow and served before they get too crispy. They are as far from ordinary bacon as you can get and ideal for the ultimate BLT. Virginia's **Edwards** makes an excellent bacon from Berkshire-breed pigs that is like having bacon taken to a higher power. All of these purveyors are easily found online, and while they are more expensive than your regular sale brand, they are in another class.

They all offer the bacon in slabs, so you can cut your own slices any thickness you want, and the slabs are great for making bacon dice for salads or chowders. Cooking sliced bacon in your oven at 350° on a rack over a foil-covered pan is the best way to cook bacon to crispy perfection. If you have never tried a slow-roasted piece of thickly sliced (1/4-inch or so) bacon, you are missing a vital piece of the pork experience. Roasting a larger slab of bacon topped with AURAS Spice Mix and brown sugar until it is caramelized on top and crispy at the edges—about 30 minutes—is an easy way to cook bacon for a crowd, although the result is not the crisp strip most people expect, and is more like pork belly.

Finally, when it comes to sausage, **Edwards Smoked Sausage Links** are the best anywhere. Deeply savory with strong sage notes, it keeps well in the freezer and can be cooked straight from frozen. It benefits from a traditional pan steaming and frying to plump up perfectly, and the result is an excellent accompaniment to the Shrimp and Grits on page 33.

Juiciest Hamburgers Two Ways

SERVES 6

THE SECRET TO A GREAT HAMBURGER IS FAT AND SPACE. Ultra-lean burgers are dry and tasteless, so use ground chuck—a nice 20% fat grind that is full of flavor. You can even add fat to improve leaner cuts like sirloin or round. Adding a few tablespoons of bacon fat or butter can vastly improve the taste of leaner cuts.

THE SECOND ESSENTIAL FOR A GOOD BURGER IS *NOT* COMPACTING THE MEAT. A lot of pressing and handling will make the hamburger dry. Treating the freshly ground meat gently—adding nothing to it but seasoning on the outside—will make a juicy burger every time. Gentle handling is easy to see; you should be able to recognize the original pattern of the grind in your finished patties. If they've been pressed into oblivion, so have all the pockets of space needed for fat and juices to be trapped as the burgers cook.

COOKING A BURGER OVER COALS AND ON A FLAT-TOP GRILL ARE TWO ENTIRELY DIFFERENT EXPERIENCES. On the grill, thicker, rounded burgers benefit from the extreme heat of the coals, where they form a crusty exterior sear and a moist interior as the juices steam inside. On a griddle, cooking in their own fat produces a crunchy exterior, and the insides stay juicy while cooking to a greater degree of doneness.

- **2 lbs** freshly ground chuck
- **3 Tbs** AURAS Spice Mix (page 9)
- **4 Tbs** butter (on griddle)
- **6** brioche buns, split

On a Grill

Gently separate ground chuck into 6 portions, using as little pressure as possible. Gently form meat into balls, then press to flatten into irregular disks. Meat should be loose and just holding together. The burgers should be 1½ inches thick and 4 inches wide. Make a 1/2-inch indentation in the top center with your thumb so that the inside center will cook evenly with the rest. Sprinkle both sides generously with spice mix.

Heat coals in a chimney, then pour into one side of a grill and position rack. Allow several minutes for the rack to become very hot. Gently place burgers on rack, and cover with grill lid. Leave them alone for 2 minutes. Remove lid and attempt to turn with spatula. If burgers stick, let cook another minute until they release. Turn burgers and cover; cook for 3 more minutes for medium. For cheeseburgers, lift lid after 2 minutes on second side and add cheese; replace lid and cook for 1 more minute. Serve immediately.

On a Griddle

Gently separate ground chuck into 6 portions. Using fingertips, flatten without compacting each burger to an irregular disk shape, about 5 inches wide and 2/3 inch thick. Sprinkle generously with spice mix. Using a medium-hot smooth griddle or 12-inch skillet, divide butter into 6 pieces to melt in pan where you will place each burger. When butter foams, put burgers on top and allow to cook until edges are crispy, about 2 minutes. Flip burgers and continue cooking for 2 more minutes for medium. For cheeseburgers, after flipping burgers, cook for 1 minute; then add cheese. Cover with a tall pot lid or aluminum bowl with a handle and allow to cook for 2 more minutes. Serve immediately.

The Total Experience

Cooking a great hamburger is just the start of the experience. Every burger deserves a great roll. A soft, thick bun such as a potato roll or brioche is the perfect complement to a juicy hamburger, whereas the often wimpy rolls labeled for hamburgers are too thin and small to stand up to burgers of this heft. Good buns are even better when they are buttered and toasted on the grill, adding some crunch to the experience. Lettuce, tomato, bacon, pickles, ketchup, mustard, and mayo may be the American basics, but they are clearly just the beginning. Whatever you choose, the best way to make your great burger combo is to put the add-ons *under* the burger and the condiments on the top. That way, all the juices work their way into the extras, not into your hands. A little preparation goes a long way. Cutting add-ons to bun-size pieces, cutting and braiding bacon to fit a bun before cooking, or prepping the cheese in a perfect pile for the final melt all help contribute to the ultimate hamburger experience.

Layered Omelet

SERVES 1

3	eggs
1 Tbs	butter
1 Tbs	cream
1/4 tsp	salt
1 Tbs	shallot, minced
1/2 tsp	tarragon
1/2 cup	fresh baby spinach
3 Tbs	Gruyère, shredded
2 Tbs	sour cream

Heat a 12-inch nonstick skillet on medium-high heat. Crack eggs and combine in a measuring cup with tarragon, salt, and cream; whisk vigorously to combine. Add butter to heated pan and move around to coat the bottom.

Add shallot and spinach and cook down, about 1-2 minutes, until spinach is wilted and darker green but not entirely limp. Pour egg mixture into pan and spread around completely by shaking pan vigorously, forming a large, thin layer. Immediately tilt pan to allow liquid egg mixture to slide under cooked egg until entire surface is evenly wet and beginning to congeal, about 1 minute.

Add Gruyère evenly over surface; spread the sour cream thinly in the middle of the eggs. Start to fold the omelet, folding outside edges about 3 inches toward the center on three sides to form a square shape. Then starting at the side closest to the handle, fold the egg over in 2-inch increments across the pan toward the far side. When there is only one fold remaining, finish by folding the last edge in the opposite direction over the eggs.

MAKING AN OMELET THIS WAY PRODUCES A MULTI-LAYERED INTERIOR WITH FILLING IN EVERY BITE. Who says that omelets have to have their filling on the inside? Once you taste this version, made with fresh, quickly wilted baby spinach, you will never order a conventional spinach omelet again. Although they start on the bottom of the pan, the spinach and shallots will end up "inside" the omelet when you are finished.

THE FOLDING TECHNIQUE HERE ALLOWS THE CENTER TO FINISH WHILE THE FIRST FOLDS ARE MADE. The gist of the technique is to pour and fold the egg within a minute. The hot skillet will cook the egg quickly, so the most vital elements are a good non-stick pan and a thin, wide spatula. The folds should be no more than 3 inches on each side so that when you begin to create the rolling fold toward the far corner, you end up turning it three more times before you flip the other end over the rest of the egg. Your omelet will have five or six layers inside.

If it seems a little like origami, it's because this is based in part on a Japanese rolled omelet, which achieves the same multiple layers by sequentially adding three thin layers of egg in a square pan and rolling them up into a large oblong roll that is like an egg log.

THERE ARE LOTS OF ALTERNATIVES TO THE SPINACH-SHALLOT-GRUYÈRE INGREDIENTS IN THIS VERSION. But they all work the same way: put the veggies in first and allow them to reduce. Mushrooms, scallions, zucchini, fresh basil leaves, and tomatoes are good choices. Just make sure they are cut very thin so they cook quickly in the foaming butter.

YOU CAN ALSO EXPERIMENT WITH THE CHEESES. Fresh goat cheese crumbled over the egg is a tangy filling, and sprinkling Parmesan over the omelet as it cooks is so good it doesn't need any additional ingredients.

FINALLY, GARNISHES THAT ACCOMPANY THE OMELET REALLY ADD TO THE ENJOYMENT. Sliced avocado, cubed fresh tomato, or a salsa all add complexity to the presentation. For a special treat, try adding the Avocado Coulis that accompanies the swordfish recipe on page 17.

Asian Mussel Soup

SERVES 6

OFTEN, THE BEST PART OF A BOWL OF STEAMED MUSSELS IS THE BROTH CREATED DURING THE PROCESS OF STEAMING. If you'd rather enjoy your mussels steamed, chow down, but save 12 or so for garnish in the soup. Return the discarded shells and broth to the pot and bring to a boil for a minute before adding the rest of the ingredients and continuing with the recipe. That way, you can have your mussels and eat soup, too.

An elegant way to serve this soup is to strain the solids from the stock and reserve while making the soup. Then, place a serving of the vegetables in a small pile in the center of the soup bowl, add some mussels on top, and ladle the soup from a tureen (or pour from a pitcher) around them.

- **2 lbs** cultivated live mussels, beards removed if necessary
- **3 Tbs** olive oil
- **1½ cups** dry white wine
- **13 oz** coconut milk (1 can)
- **1 cup** water
- **1** medium onion, coarsely chopped
- **2** garlic cloves, minced
- **2 Tbs** fresh ginger, julienned
- **1 cup** fennel, julienned
- **1 cup** carrot, julienned
- **1 cup** red and yellow peppers, julienned
- **1** small jalapeno, seeded and cut into small julienne
- **1/2 cup** cilantro, chopped
- **1/4 cup** lime juice
- **2 Tbs** fish sauce
- **2 oz** Thai red curry paste (Maesri brand)
- **1 tsp** salt (or to taste)
- **2 Tbs** butter
- **2 Tbs** flour
- **1 cup** whole milk

Heat an 8-quart Dutch oven over high heat. Add oil and heat until it shimmers. Add onion and cook until transparent, 2 minutes. Add garlic and cook until fragrant, about 1 minute. Add ginger, fennel, carrot, red pepper, and jalapeno; sauté until soft, about 2 minutes. Dump mussels into the pot and add white wine. Cover pot and let mussels steam for 3 minutes. Stir mussels and cook another 3 minutes until mussel shells have opened. Remove mussels with a slotted spoon.

Discard any mussels that have not opened; remove mussels from shells and reserve, and return shells to the pot along with any liquids. Turn down heat to simmer; add coconut milk, water, lime juice, fish sauce, salt, and curry paste; let pot simmer for 30 minutes. Remove mussel shells. Take off heat and stir in cilantro.

In a 4-quart pot, melt butter over medium-high heat until it foams, add flour and whisk into a *roux*. When *roux* is light tan and bubbling, slowly add milk while whisking until a thickened *béchamel* sauce forms. Slowly add broth from Dutch oven while stirring to create soup. Add mussels and serve with a crusty baguette.

6 CUPS

Crab Cakes with Coleslaw

SERVES 4

- **1 lb** lump bluefin crabmeat
- **8 Tbs** butter (1 stick)
- **1 tsp** salt
- **1 Tbs** Worcestershire sauce
- **1 Tbs** lemon juice
- **1/4 cup** onion, finely diced
- **1/4 cup** Italian parsley, chopped
- **2 Tbs** mayonnaise
- **1 tsp** dry mustard
- **1/2 tsp** celery salt
- **1** egg, lightly beaten
- **2 Tbs** heavy cream
- **1 cup** panko bread crumbs + 2 Tbs
- **1 cup** vegetable oil

Carefully pick through crabmeat and discard any cartilage. Break up the lumps into smaller pieces with a fork, leaving some lumps whole. Melt butter in a 10-inch skillet. When foaming subsides, add crabmeat and salt and toss to combine. Allow to cool. In a mixing bowl, combine Worcestershire sauce, lemon, onion, parsley, mayonnaise, mustard, celery salt, egg, cream, and 2 tablespoons of bread crumbs; fold to combine. Add cooled crabmeat mixture and combine well.

Put 1 cup bread crumbs in a shallow bowl. Divide crabmeat mixture into 8 balls. Roll in bread crumbs to lightly coat, and press into disks using a 3½-inch ring mold or by hand. Place in refrigerator for at least 1 hour.

Heat oil in a 10-inch skillet to 360°. Fry crabcakes 4 at a time, placing them gently in the pan and leaving alone until golden on underside, about 4 minutes, then turn gently using spatula and spoon. The cakes will be fragile but the crust should hold them together. Cook on second side another 3 minutes. Place cooked crab cakes on paper towel to drain and repeat with remaining cakes. Keep warm in a 200° oven if necessary. Serve with cocktail sauce and coleslaw.

Quick Coleslaw

SERVES 4

- **2 cups** green cabbage with some purple for color, shredded
- **1/4 cup** carrot, shredded
- **1/3 cup** mayonnaise
- **1/4 cup** lemon juice (2 small lemons)
- **2 Tbs** sugar
- **1 tsp** celery seed

Toss to combine cabbage and carrot in mixing bowl. Add remaining ingredients and thoroughly integrate into cabbage mixture. Pack tightly into container and refrigerate for at least 1 hour.

Cocktail Sauce

- **1/2 cup** ketchup
- **1/4 cup** grated horseradish
- **2 Tbs** lemon juice

Combine all ingredients and mix thoroughly. Refrigerate for 1 hour to allow flavors to bloom. For less spicy sauce, add more ketchup. For a really spicy sauce, add wasabi powder.

MARYLAND-STYLE CRAB CAKES GET A BAD RAP FROM OVERZEALOUS USE OF OLD BAY SEASONING AND TOO MUCH FILLER. These crab cakes have none of the former and only a bit of the latter. They are bound mostly by butter and a custard. Cooling formed cakes in the refrigerator until the butter solidifies again is crucial to getting the taste right when they are fried. The resulting cakes will be crisp on the outside and creamy on the inside. Using panko bread crumbs will give the crab cakes an extra hit of crunchiness. Don't worry if they get a bit soggy from their stay in the fridge; they will crunch right up in the hot oil.

NOT ALL CRABMEAT IS THE SAME. The blue crab that is the gold standard for most Maryland-style crab dishes is found along the Atlantic coast and the Gulf. Much of the crabmeat sold in big-box stores comes from Thailand, from a similar but not as tasty crab. The lumps may look luxurious, but the taste isn't the same.

THIS IS AN EASY-TO-MAKE MOUSSE that looks and tastes a lot more sophisticated than its ingredients would suggest, especially when it's served with a simple *beurre blanc* or Hollandaise sauce.

In fact, this recipe can be used with a variety of vegetables, although more substantial ones should be cooked first. Try butternut squash, corn, sweet potatoes, broccoli, or asparagus. You can even try mixing two in one dish. Prepare them separately and spoon them, one on top of the other, into the dishes, allowing a short rest between layers. The plated results are impressive.

TO REALLY GO FOR THE GUSTO, MAKE THIS A SOUFFLÉ INSTEAD OF A MOUSSE by eliminating half the cream and separating the yolks and whites of the eggs. Mix all ingredients except egg whites. Whip whites into soft peaks and then fold into yolk mixture, then proceed without the water bath. The soufflés take 20–30 minutes and will rise, so they need to be made in separate ramekins rather than a muffin tin, because they won't be aerated.

Champagne Beurre Blanc

MAKES 1 CUP

- **2** shallots, finely chopped
- **1/4 cup** Champagne vinegar
- **1/4 cup** white wine
- **3 Tbs** heavy cream
- **8 Tbs** butter, cut into 16 pieces
- salt and cayenne pepper to taste

In a small saucepan, slowly reduce vinegar and white wine with shallots until nearly dry. Over medium heat, add heavy cream and butter, adding the butter a piece at a time and whisking constantly until butter is melted, emulsified, and warm. Be careful not to heat this to a boil, or it will break. Season to taste with salt and a pinch of cayenne pepper. The sauce will hold in a warm water bath for several hours.

Spinach Timbale

SERVES 6

- **1 lb** fresh spinach
- **1** shallot, minced
- **4** eggs
- **1 cup** heavy cream
- **1/2 tsp** salt
- **1/8 tsp** nutmeg

Bring pot of water to boil. Rinse spinach if needed and toss in batches to blanch, about 1 minute each batch. Transfer blanched spinach to tea towel and squeeze out as much water as possible. Add spinach, shallot, salt, and eggs to a food processer and pulse 2 or 3 times to purée.

Preheat oven to 350°. In a 9×12-inch baking dish, add hot water to fill halfway, to be used as a water bath.

Prepare 6-ounce timbale dishes, ramekins, or, if you don't have those, a muffin pan, by putting a piece of parchment on the bottom of each section and spraying with cooking spray. Spoon the mixture into dishes. Sprinkle nutmeg on top and place into the baking pan water bath. Place in oven for 30–40 minutes. The spinach timbales will rise and the tops will darken. Timbales are done when a toothpick comes out clean. To extract, run a knife around the edges; put a plate over each container (or baking sheet over muffin pan); invert, and remove parchment. Spoon Champagne Beurre Blanc around the base of each timbale.

Simplest Tomato Soup

SERVES 4

- **4** large ripe tomatoes, halved and crosshatched on bottom and top
- **4 Tbs** butter
- **1 cup** cream
- **1 cup** milk
- **1/4 tsp** Italian seasoning
- **1/2 tsp** salt
- **1 Tbs** Parmesan

In a 12-inch skillet, add butter and heat over medium heat until foaming subsides. Add tomatoes, cut side down, and cook for 5 minutes until tomatoes begin to caramelize on the bottom and render juices. Turn over and continue cooking another 3 minutes or until tomatoes soften and begin to disintegrate. Add remaining ingredients and continue cooking. Using the side of a spatula or spoon, break up pieces of tomato until all the elements have combined. Soup should be a light red color with chunks of tomato. Serve immediately.

IF YOU LOVE TOMATOES AT THE PEAK OF THE SEASON, this is the most satisfying soup you will ever eat. Served with a salad, it makes a fabulous light meal and is the perfect *al fresco* menu for a summer evening. And it goes without saying that it is the perfect accompaniment for the Ultimate Grilled Cheese.

Ultimate Grilled Cheese

SERVES 1

- **2 slices** brioche or challah, cut thick
- **3 Tbs** unsalted butter, softened
- **1 oz** sharp Cheddar, sliced into thin strips
- **1 oz** Brie, softened at room temperature
- **1 oz** Gruyère, shredded
- **1 slice** thin-cut bacon, cut into 2 pieces

In a 10-inch nonstick skillet, cook bacon until crisp over medium heat. Clean pan.

On one slice of bread, distribute the Brie in small pieces, and top with the bacon. Next, place shredded Gruyère over the bacon. Finally, add thin pieces of Cheddar evenly over the rest. Position the second slice of bread to complete the sandwich. Spread half of the butter thickly on the top piece of bread.

Heat skillet to medium-low. Melt remaining butter in pan and place sandwich, buttered side up, on top of melted butter, moving bread around pan to coat crusts. Cook slowly, 5-6 minutes, until bottom crust is golden, butter is absorbed, and cheese has begun to melt. Carefully flip sandwich. Cook second side until golden and cheese has completely melted, another 4 minutes or so. Avoid pressing down on sandwich.

Cut sandwich diagonally and serve with Simplest Tomato Soup.

EACH OF THE THREE CHEESES ADDS ITS SPECIAL NOTE TO THIS SANDWICH. The trick is preparing them so they all melt evenly. Cooking the sandwich over a medium-low heat allows the bread to absorb the butter and turn golden while the cheeses melt. The bacon, especially if it is one of the three brands described on page 49, adds the complete savory experience.

Or, just use any kind of bread and three slices of American cheese, because when it comes to a grilled cheese sandwich, nothing is as satisfying as this gooey memory of childhood.

THIS MARYLAND-STYLE FRIED CHICKEN IS COATED IN A FLOUR MIXTURE, NOT BREADING. The salty, sour buttermilk brines the chicken and provides a base for the flour to stick to. Double coating makes a thick crust that encases the meat; if you like a thinner crust, just dip and coat once. But be careful to cover the entire piece. Breaches in the coating will allow oil to seep into the chicken, making it greasy, not juicy. Resting the chicken for at least 30 minutes before frying is the secret to getting the most perfect combination of crisp crust and moist meat.

THE CHICKEN IS PAN-FRIED IN 2 CUPS OF OIL, INSTEAD OF THE USUAL 6 TO 8 CUPS in a Dutch oven, and then finished in the oven, which sheds excess oil and crisps the crust. You can fry the chicken in the conventional manner, and cook submerged for 15–20 minutes until done, or you can avoid the frying altogether and cook the chicken for 30–40 minutes in the oven, but the final result will be dryer chicken and less crunchy skin.

Health-conscious people might want to tear off the breading and skin, and they will find juicy moist chicken. For traditionalists, the combination of crust, skin and meat is worth the extra calories. This chicken is also great served cold the next day.

Pan-Fried Chicken

SERVES 6

- **4** breasts, bone-in and skin-on
- **4** thighs, bone-in and skin-on
- **8** legs, bone-in and skin-on
- **4 cups** buttermilk
- **1/4 cup** table salt
- **1 cup** flour
- **1/4 cup** AURAS Spice Mix (page 9)
- **1/2 tsp** cayenne pepper
- **2 Tbs** sugar
- **2 Tbs** cornstarch
- **2 cups** vegetable oil

Add salt to the buttermilk and stir to combine. Rinse chicken parts; trim any straggly ends; soak in buttermilk for at least 1 hour, preferably 3 hours. Mix flour, spice mix, cayenne, sugar and cornstarch together in deep mixing bowl. Take chicken from buttermilk; shake off excess; and dredge chicken, 1 piece at a time, through flour mixture by placing in center of deep bowl and vigorously swirling the bowl to coat the chicken. Re-dip the chicken in the buttermilk and dredge again to make a thick coating. Place on piece of aluminum foil to dry. Repeat with remaining pieces. Let chicken rest for 30 minutes before frying to allow coating to dry.

Preheat oven to 375°. Prepare a baking pan with rack by covering the pan under the rack with foil.

Over high heat, bring oil in a 12-inch cast iron sauté pan to 360°. Using tongs, place 3 or 4 pieces of chicken in oil to cook, being careful not to crowd the pan. Fry without moving for 2 minutes, then check that chicken is not sticking to bottom. If it is, use edge of tongs to gently dislodge. After another minute or so, when chicken is lightly golden, flip to other side. Cook another 3 minutes until coating has turned a light brown on both sides. Move chicken to rack and repeat with remaining pieces.

After all the meat is fried, transfer tray to center of oven and cook for 15 minutes or until instant-read thermometer in thigh reads 170°. Serve immediately or keep warm in 200° oven.

Vegetable Gratin

SERVES 4

- **2 Tbs** olive oil
- **1/4 cup** dry white wine
- **1 Tbs** soy sauce
- **1** sweet onion, cut pole-to-pole into 1/2-inch pieces
- **4** garlic cloves, sliced thin
- **4 oz** white or cremini mushrooms, sliced into 1/2-inch pieces
- **1** red pepper, julienned
- **1/2 cup** fennel, cut into 1/2-inch julienne
- **1/2 lb** cauliflower and broccoli, broken into small florets
- **1/2 lb** string beans, cut into 2-inch segments
- **3** carrots, julienned
- **2** medium zucchini, quartered lengthwise, cut into 1/2-inch pieces
- **1 tsp** thyme (or 1 Tbs fresh)
- **1 tsp** rosemary (or 1 Tbs fresh)
- **1 tsp** oregano (or 1 Tbs fresh)
- **1 tsp** salt
- **8 oz** fresh mozzarella, cubed
- **1/2 cup** Parmesan, grated and divided
- **2/3 cup** heavy cream
- **1/4 cup** bread crumbs

Preheat oven to 400°. Prepare all the ingredients before starting, placing each into its own cup or bowl. The herbs can be mixed together. Heat oil in a 12-inch sauté pan over high heat. Add onions and fennel, then sprinkle herbs over them. Sauté until onions begin to brown on edges; add mushrooms and garlic. Continue to sauté over high heat until mushrooms begin to render liquid and brown on the edges, about 6 minutes. Add soy sauce and stir to coat, cooking for 1 more minute. Add white wine and dissolve *fond* at bottom of pan. Turn down heat to medium; add remaining vegetables except zucchini, sauté quickly to combine; cover pan and cook for 8 minutes or until vegetables begin to soften. Add zucchini, stirring to combine, and continue cooking for another 3 minutes.

Transfer pan contents to a large bowl. Stir in salt and 1/4 cup of the Parmesan. Fold in cubed mozzarella and distribute evenly. Using a large spoon, decant mixture into four 20-ounce ramekins or gratin dishes, gently compressing the vegetables into the bowls. Add 3 tablespoons of cream to each. Combine remaining Parmesan with bread crumbs and sprinkle to cover tops. Transfer ramekins to middle rack of oven, and cook until topping browns and gratin bubbles, about 12 minutes.

Serve the gratin right in the ramekins, or decant onto a plate or large bowl.

A GRATIN IS JUST A CASSEROLE THAT USES CREAM AND CHEESE and whatever vegetables or starches are available. In a way, mac-and-cheese is just another gratin, albeit a really saucy one. This gratin is filling enough as a main course; in smaller containers, it makes for a great side dish.

This dish is very flexible. Try using different vegetables such as asparagus, snap peas, corn, Brussels sprouts, bok choy or leeks—really, all vegetables work, provided they are added in an order that renders them cooked well at the end. Aromatics go in first, mushrooms next, tough veggies next and tender veggies last.

YOU CAN ADD PROTEIN TO THIS GRATIN, TOO. Cubed, precooked chicken breast or raw shrimp are great additions, provided they are cut or cubed into bite-sized pieces. The shrimp can go in with the last veggies and will be perfectly cooked when they come out of the oven.

For a more savory flavor, add 2 strips of thick-cut bacon diced into 1/4-inch pieces at the start with the oil. Reserve the cooked bacon and sprinkle it on the gratin before you add the topping.

Finally, the gratin reheats well in the microwave, so make a few extra servings.

Shirred Eggs in Two Sauces

SERVES 4

BAKED OR SHIRRED EGGS ARE AN ELEGANT WAY TO MAKE A BRUNCH FOR A LOT OF PEOPLE, provided you have enough ramekins. It's easy to extend these recipes, and the mixtures can be made ahead and added together at the last moment. The tomato version is more assertively acidic and pairs well with grits or hash browns. The more traditional spinach and mushroom version has a cream base; it's important to have the eggs at room temperature and to warm the cream so that the eggs will cook properly. Gauging their doneness is the tricky part of the process. Opening channels in the mixture to allow the whites to spread will make it easier for the whites to finish while the yolks are still runny.

Tomato Mélange

- **8** eggs at room temperature
- **4** slices thick bacon, diced
- **2** large shallots, diced
- **1** large onion, diced
- **1 cup** tomatoes, coarsely chopped
- **1 tsp** salt
- **1/2 tsp** thyme (or 1/2 Tbs fresh)
- **1/2 tsp** tarragon (or 1 Tbs fresh)
- **2 Tbs** lemon juice
- **4 tsp** balsamic vinegar
- **dash** hot sauce (or to taste)
- **4 oz** Gruyère, shredded

Preheat oven to 350°. Crack two eggs into each of four bowls (you won't be cooking in these) and reserve.

Place bacon in a 12-inch sauté pan over medium heat, stir to separate pieces and cook until crisp. Using a slotted spoon, remove and reserve bacon. Add shallot, onion, and spices and cook until softened, about 5 minutes.

Add tomatoes and salt, stirring to combine, and cover pan. Cook until tomatoes just begin to break down, about 4 minutes. Add lemon juice and balsamic vinegar, and continue to cook for another minute until mixture has the consistency of fresh salsa.

Divide tomato mixture into four shallow 13-ounce ovenproof dishes or ramekins. Using a spoon, push the mixture to the edges of the dish, opening a space in the center. Pour two eggs from each bowl into each ramekin; add salt and pepper to taste; sprinkle shredded Gruyère lightly around eggs, leaving them uncovered; sprinkle bacon over mixture. Cook for 12 minutes until whites are almost set and eggs are runny, or to taste. The eggs will be slightly undercooked, but they will finish out of the oven in another few minutes. Serve in the dishes.

Spinach Mushroom

- **8** eggs at room temperature
- **1 lb** baby spinach
- **3 Tbs** olive oil
- **2** large shallots, diced
- **8 oz** baby bella mushrooms, sliced
- **1/2 tsp** rosemary (or 1/2 Tbs fresh)
- **1/2 tsp** thyme (or 1 Tbs fresh)
- **12** fresh basil leaves (do not use dried)
- **1 tsp** salt
- **3/4 cup** cream, warmed
- **4 oz** Cheddar, shredded

Preheat oven to 350°. Crack two eggs into each of four bowls (you won't be cooking in these) and reserve.

In a 12-inch sauté pan, heat olive oil to shimmer. Add shallots and cook until transparent, about 1 minute. Add spices and allow to bloom, about 30 seconds. Add mushrooms and cook until all liquid is rendered and mushrooms are browned on edges, about 5 minutes.

Add spinach to pan and cook until wilted. Add salt and stir; take off heat and allow to cool for a few minutes. Divide mixture into four shallow, 10-ounce, ovenproof dishes or ramekins. Using a spoon, push the mixture to the edges of the dish, opening a space in the center. Pour the eggs from each bowl into the center of each ramekin; add salt and pepper to taste.

Pour 3 tablespoons of warmed cream over spinach mushroom mixture; then sprinkle shredded Cheddar lightly around eggs, leaving them uncovered, and place in oven. Cook for 12 minutes until whites are almost set and eggs are runny, or to taste. The eggs will be undercooked, but they will finish out of the oven in another few minutes. Serve in the dishes.

A Personal History of AURAS Design

BY ROBERT SUGAR/FOUNDER & CREATIVE DIRECTOR

IT'S HARD TO SEPARATE the story of AURAS from my own history. I have always wanted to be a graphic designer. I remember drawing Chevrolet chevrons in kindergarten. Throughout my school years, if there was any assignment that could be augmented with drawings or comic strips, that's what I'd do.

In high school, I took print shop instead of calculus—a move that landed me a session with the principal, who wanted to know why I was hanging with the trade-school kids instead of the ivy-league-bound SAT stars. But print shop proved to be very useful. I learned about prepress and typesetting (which in those days actually involved putting metal type into a chase) and began to produce design projects.

The author in 1988—already going gray.

I have always tried to make AURAS a place where I would want to work and to be the kind of generous creative director who would teach and inspire rather than micromanage. I learned a lot from the bosses and workplaces of my early experiences in the field.

MY FIRST "REAL" JOB, working at a print shop called Colortone Press, began with a humbling event. The owner, Al Hackle, was too cheap to have reset entire lines of type for the old mechanicals he wanted updated. Instead, he would have a hot-type vendor set small numbers and codes to be mortised into the old paste-ups—a tedious and exacting job that was really too meticulous for my nascent paste-up skills. Nevertheless, I knew the basics, and with great bravado, fed the type through the sheet waxer, only to realize I'd run it upside down. A goof, sure, but I knew a little solvent would take the wax right off. However, I'd only encountered phototype sheets, not hot-type copy made by inking the hot metal typeset lines on a proof press. The solvent dissolved the wax and also, to my horror, smeared the type beyond use. The production manager, an easy-going guy named Bill Meadows, gave me a huge amount of static—wondering who was going to pay to have it all reset—until he produced another proof sheet from the typesetter. Of course, little did I know that they sent multiple sets of copy for just such occurrences. I learned a valuable lesson—never claim to know how to do something when you just *think* you know how to do it.

Al Hackle loved printing and encouraged me to go through the plant and learn all I could. From camera room to stripping, platemaking to press, folding to binding, each part of producing a printed product had its own set of tools, skills and language. Most designers didn't have a clue how their creations were printed, but it became clear to me that if you didn't understand the total process, you weren't as likely to get a good final piece.

Printers preferred to let designers believe they knew how to paste up their own boards. After receiving the mechanicals (original art shot for the negatives that would become part of the print process) from the designer, a printer would often completely redo them before shooting the film but let the designer take credit for making beautiful paste-ups. Just like high school print shop, the world of design and printing was a class-stratified system where design people and production people did their jobs and hardly interacted. When they did, the pecking order was clear: the designers were clients (thus always right) and the printers were vendors.

After Colortone, I spent most of my college years working at the American Chemical Society in its in-house design and production department. Working freelance (but nearly full-time) at ACS was a great way to learn the ins and outs of producing magazines. At the time—in the late 1970s—ACS produced five titles. I worked on them all—sometimes just creating charts and graphs, but sometimes getting to design.

One of the best perks about working at ACS was being allowed to work on other freelance jobs during off hours and get feedback from the other designers.

The department was run by Leroy Corcoran. He taught me a lot about managing a studio. He gave people opportunities to grow and accepted mistakes as part of the job, not failures of character. He fostered a sense of camaraderie among his employees and was always willing to pitch in when things needed to get done. To me, working at ACS was an extension of my college education. I was going to American University and majoring in communications and design, but often it seemed I learned a lot more outside the classroom.

To this day, I appreciate the way Leroy managed his department. He protected his people from the politics and hassles in the rest of the organization, and he stood up for them when they faced unreasonable demands from other departments. He had designers work directly with the "clients" in other departments, allowing them to take ownership of their work, build relationships, and improve communication skills.

All these experiences informed my sense of what a design studio should be. I thought that, when the time came, I could have a place where creative people enjoyed coming to work and were challenged by dealing directly with clients.

MY FIRST PAYING MAGAZINE CLIENT was the result of an exasperated designer who wanted to get rid of a client—a novice publisher who bristled at paying the outrageous sum of *six dollars a page* for layout and design. The designer, Judy Mays, had hired me to help paste up technical books and figured that, as a newly minted designer still in college, I would be happy with whatever work I could get. That is how I started working for Hershel Shanks and his Biblical Archaeology Society.

In the beginning, I may have been only a few steps ahead of Hershel's knowledge about magazine design, but they were crucial steps. When I proved that an 8½×11 magazine with a color picture on the cover could be printed for the same price as his current 7×10 book, he allowed me to do my first redesign. Ultimately, his little project grew to four magazines, and BAS remains a client after 30 years. Every business needs a pivotal client, and Hershel was mine. He can be abrupt and stubborn, with a ready-fire-aim problem-solving technique (once he decreed that letters were never ever supposed to "touch" in headlines). But he has always been loyal and supportive of me and my studio. At this point, ours is far beyond the usual business relationship.

In the early days, Hershel was constantly looking for better deals in producing his magazine, and changed printers and typesetters with upsetting frequency. However, after a small typesetting firm—one that didn't waste money on things like backup punch tapes—produced an entire issue's worth of typesetting that slowly began to fade a day after it was delivered, he finally agreed to deal with a more reputable typesetting firm. BAS used Harwood Type for four years, and I spent many hours at Harwood's watching Harry Woodell and Tom Nevins set type on their Quaddex system. Along the way, I learned a lot about typesetting.

This all started while I was still in

college, and I found ways of using my emerging design skills on campus. The biggest challenge I undertook was becoming yearbook editor. It wasn't hard to become editor; it was a position with no other takers. While it was a ridiculous amount of work to add to my schedule, it was a chance to create a book! As both editor and designer, I had my first opportunity to hold creative control over both the look and content of a big printed piece. It is an addicting experience, and it confirmed something that I have always believed: design serves content, and the perfect solution to any design problem is, at core, finding a better way of telling a story or explaining an idea.

I graduated from AU in 1978 and kept freelancing at ACS. After a while, the "non-ACS" work was getting to be too much of an imposition on the generosity of Leroy, who only very gently complained. I knew I had to start my own studio and stop using ACS as a crutch. In 1981 I started AURAS Design in a corner of my apartment. The name comes from Latin and, loosely translated, means "you are gold," but it also kind of sounds like my initials, and at the time it was trendy to have obscure single-word studio names. AURAS seemed a perfect choice.

As most who have worked out of their home might agree, after a while it feels like you'll go insane if you do it one day longer. I'd find excuses to head to ACS to visit with the crew there, or walk around the nearby National Zoo. One thing I realized—you never want to make your home a place you dread. I needed to find a real office space. Eventually, one of my new clients, a PR firm called Sobus & Lane, invited me to share space and be its in-house design partner. They seemed like smart people, so I agreed. We found space on Cathedral Avenue in an apartment building that backed up to the zoo. In the summer, when the wind blew just so, you knew you were near the animals.

After we—AURAS (just me) and four of them—moved into a two-bedroom apartment, things started to get weird. To my admittedly naive sense of business conduct, they all seemed a little too friendly, but as it turned out, it was much weirder—they were all deep into EST. Erhard Seminar Training might be lost to time today, but back then it had gained a following. It was sort of a cross between Scientology and Mary Kay Cosmetics.

They seemed certain that by using their EST training, they would become a highly successful firm. In reality, all they did was annoy and alienate their clients, and after a few months I had the apartment on Cathedral Avenue to myself. By the end of 1981 EST was history, too.

Over the next few years, I had a variety of office mates; the best was Lauren Wadsworth, a new age-y masseuse who set up her practice in the other bedroom "office." One of the side benefits of the arrangement was getting a weekly massage.

My first attempt at hiring an employee was a disaster—a woman who, as it turned out, had not been honest about her portfolio or her skill set. My first "real" employee, Mariann Seriff, proved to me that it was indeed possible to find a good designer who knew how to design. Soon we added a few new clients and a few more designers; business was starting to take off.

ONE DAY I RECEIVED A NOTICE from the D.C. government that my business was going to be audited. I was completely unprepared for the event and had made a major mistake: I hadn't realized that a design firm had to charge sales tax on its work. The auditor presented an initial estimate that I owed the District of Columbia over $40,000 in back sales tax. I had to show that my clients were exempt because they were either nonprofits or not based in D.C.

The biggest help fixing the situation came from a modern dancer I had met while photographing a group called the Dance Exchange. Helen Rea wasn't just a dancer. She was in training to practice The Alexander Technique—and was also a bookkeeper. She helped me plow through my records and ultimately we proved that all but $6,000 was tax-exempt. The District sent a confirmation of our very detailed report and indicated a bill would follow. In fact, no bill came, and I never heard from them again.

We decided to incorporate AURAS Design, and start our books fresh, paying proper attention to tax billing. I had found a friend and partner in Helen, and became one of her "guinea pig" clients in her Alexander training. After a few sessions, she helped relieve a back problem that I had endured for years. Soon we grew into a real couple, and her contributions to making AURAS successful throughout the years are beyond measure.

I ALWAYS FELT THAT AURAS SHOULD be a place where the resources were used for creative purposes. We are probably the only design studio in the country that ever created and produced a modern dance concert. I was very involved in the modern dance community and had created promotional materials and shot stills for many dance companies. When I decided to produce a concert, I had lots of chits to call in. The concert was a series of dance parodies and tongue-in-cheek performance art. It was a great opportunity to use our design skills creating short videos as well as the promotion and branding for a show. "See This Concert and Keep the Flashlight FREE" featured many well-known local dancers and was performed at The Dance Place, so it was no wonder it sold out and even got pretty decent reviews. *The Washington Post* said it was an event "that should be held every year."

THE FIRST MACINTOSH was introduced in 1984 and brought the world MacWrite and MacPaint. The Mac was a fun toy, but hardly a serious design tool. That changed in 1987, when Apple introduced the Mac II and—more important—the Laserwriter. The Laserwriter drew text using Postscript page-description language and was capable of producing type that rivaled the quality of typesetting machines—although most typesetters didn't want to believe it. Unlike every system that preceded it, Postscript type was based on vectors, not bitmaps, so it could be any size—from a small footnote to a huge headline—and still be razor sharp, or at least as sharp as its 300 dpi resolution would allow.

Mariann was positive that AURAS was way behind the curve adopting computers. So on the day before Christmas in 1987, I ordered our first Mac II and a ridiculously expensive Ikegami monitor—4,000 bucks and it mostly sucked. (I regretted not spending *six grand* on a Sony Trinitron for years afterward). But I was so sure the Mac II wouldn't be a useful tool that I didn't even bother buying a printer. The day after Christmas, I came to the studio to find a stack of boxes.

I had absolutely no experience setting up or using computers of any sort, so I was astounded that after attaching all the plugs and cables and turning the thing on, I heard the now-familiar chime.

Our "powerful" computer ran a copy of Aldus PageMaker 1.2 and FreeHand 1.0, and the Mac came with fonts that would print on a Laserwriter. It only took an hour or so using PageMaker for my experiences at Colortone Press and Harwood Type to tell me this wasn't just a design tool, it was a production tool—and one that would change everything about the way we worked. Learning to use the Mac was a challenge, but our initial idea of using it experimentally didn't last long.

I ordered a printer almost immediately, and, to my delight, it arrived the very next day—another new experience that was going to become a part of our everyday lives.

We produced our first live job on the computer two weeks after we got the equipment. True, it was a small brochure, and a few years later, when we looked at the file to revise it, we found it was made pretty badly, but WYSIWYG ("What You See Is What You Get") worked—it looked and printed just fine. I sent a comp of the design to the client, who promptly called me to complain that the copy wasn't finished yet, and I shouldn't have sent it to the typesetter. She needed some extra reassurance that what I had sent over was, in fact, a mere comp. That was a pretty convincing conversation about the potential of using the Mac.

Of course, Mariann was totally wrong about one thing: it didn't take long for us to realize that almost no other design firm had Macs, or knew their potential. That gave AURAS an advantage that we leveraged for many years.

AURAS HAD GROWN TO FOUR PEOPLE by the late 1980s, and we knew that the time had come to find real office space instead of squatting in a residential apartment building.

By then I was living in the Adams Morgan section of Washington, D.C., and I noticed a house for sale on Kalorama Road that I knew was zoned commercial—although it was offered as a residence.

Helen and I, carrying our new baby, Rebecca (we got married somewhere in there), wandered over for a look. The row house was a badly neglected property that had seen years of transient renters, and the current group had carved out four apartments in the small building, including the unfinished basement. The house, built in 1902, still had original gas fixtures that were installed along with electric wiring, because back then a lot of people thought that electricity might be just a passing fad. The rear of the building sagged by almost a foot, giving the floor a slant that a ball would roll down. While the structure was once a nice example of middle-class housing, with 10-foot ceilings, plaster-and-lath walls, tiled entryways and mahogany trim, it had become a sad mess.

Walking away, I said, "This place is perfect," and, simultaneously, Helen said, "This place is a disaster." In reality it was neither; it was a shell waiting for renovation at a price that was affordable and in a great location. I'd always wanted a townhouse studio that felt as comfortable as being at home. It was also a block away from where we lived. Nice commute.

Even with the cost of renovating, the monthly payment was only about $850—$300 *less* than the Cathedral Avenue space. It always seemed to me that money spent on rent was a lost asset that owning a building could remedy. And while we didn't need the huge 2,100 square feet of space yet, we could rent out the basement and grow into the building over time.

We hired a small firm to do the renovation, and, as layers of poor amateur additions were stripped away, it became apparent that the job was going to be a lot bigger than it looked. The building sagged because it was supported in the basement by two ancient railroad ties perched on brick tiers. As the ties had slowly disintegrated, the entire structure had sagged with them. The solution was to raise the entire house on jacks, replace the old wooden ties with steel, and straighten every floor joist with a new cement base.

We restored pocket doors and a fireplace mantle, and saved the floors, but ultimately, everything else in the small building was replaced. The original front door was recreated at a woodworking shop just up the street. New HVAC, plumbing and wiring were added. Drywall replaced the rotting plaster and lath. New appliances, tile and fixtures were put in the bathrooms. We added a skylight in the stairwell and replaced all the windows. In the back, we planned a large sliding glass door set among windows that spanned the entire rear wall leading to a deck.

The day the sliding door was being installed, the job foreman met me as I arrived at the building, blocking the entrance and asking: "Would you like the good news or the bad news?" That's always a troubling way to start a conversation. I chose the former, the answer to which was, "Well, no one was hurt." And the bad news? While they were adjusting the sliding doors, the entire rear wall—from the basement to the eaves—had collapsed in a cloud of dust.

For AURAS, it was actually a good thing, because the construction firm had to rebrick the entire back of the building at its own expense. Unfortunately for them, the job—one of their first—was also their last. It was only the integrity of the foreman, who came to do the punch list even though the company had gone kaput, that got the job finished.

WE MOVED INTO THE OFFICE at 1746 Kalorama Road in June 1988. During the past year we had used our computer more and more for production, but large projects were still difficult because of the lack of style sheets that could "tag" word-processing files with information that changed their font, size and leading. That changed with the release of PageMaker 2.1, installed shortly before our move. At this point we had about a dozen clients, mostly associations, and their big projects revolved around annual meetings. One client in particular, the National Association of Social Workers, had us produce a huge catalog of courses for its meeting, a project that had cost nearly $14,000 in typesetting fees the previous year.

Now, we had them tag their text and send us the entire file, instead of sending it to our typesetter. We prototyped a page, set up style sheets to match the tag names, and hit <command-D> to place the text onto the first blank page. And...nothing happened. But it was a large file, more than 120 pages of print-out. We went to lunch, and I came back early to check on the machine. To my utter amazement, there on the screen was the entire document, typeset perfectly, laid out into 80 pages. It only took a single keystroke to create a document that had previously involved 30 hours of paste-up and a huge typesetting fee.

If I wasn't already convinced that the computer was the way of the future, I was now. We used a service bureau to output perfectly laid-out pages; our total cost was $640. We billed NASW 15% less than the previous year, which made them pretty happy. Our total fee was enough to buy a second Mac system and put a down payment on our own imagesetter.

The next year we were told that NASW had been offered the same job for half our rate. Soon it was impossible to charge for typesetting, and most of the type shops in the area disappeared.

In 1990, we bought our first imagesetter, freeing us from sending files out to a service bureau. In the following decade, we bought two more generations of imagesetters. But nothing matches the thrill of your first. It took the technician

1746 Kalorama Road. The townhouse was the studio for AURAS from 1988 to 1998.

an hour to build the printer stand and 15 minutes to set it up on our network. We produced our first page of real repro a half-hour later.

Printing high-rez pages on photo paper replaced paste-up, but print shops still had to shoot halftones and strip in color separations. Our imagesetter could run film as well, and soon we were producing CMYK negatives. Unfortunately, the film would misalign as it was exposed, causing such poor registration that we'd print each page's set of negs twice and take the best four pieces of film out of eight—but it worked. The process was so new that the imagesetter's rep came to see us do it, because he was certain it was impossible to make 133-line separations on our machine. Difficult, yes, but not impossible.

In 1990, we had our turn designing and producing the Art Directors Club of Metropolitan Washington's magazine, *Full Bleed*. We decided, as a challenge, to produce an entire issue digitally. It was an alphabetical primer, each page produced by a different designer. Considering the state of the art, it's a miracle it was produced at all; today it looks primitive. But it proved to the design community that change had already arrived.

Convincing our magazine clients to switch to the Mac also took some persuasion. Our approach was to guarantee that if they weren't satisfied with the quality of the product, we would pay the typesetter the difference between our rates and theirs, usually double our fee. Not one magazine looked back after their first digitally produced issue. By the mid-1990s, we had moved entirely to digital production, and everyone had a workstation.

Eventually, nine people occupied the Kalorama studio, filling all three floors. The senior designer was—and still is—Sharri Wolfgang. She joined AURAS in 1987 after working at American Chemical Society for seven years. Sharri and I knew each other from high school. I had tried to get her to join the studio for a few years, but she wasn't quite ready to jump from the security of a big association to a small design

The second floor of Kalorama in the early '90s. We may all have gotten workstations, but they're perched on our original art tables.

firm until I had a few more steady clients.

Sharri has always tackled tough jobs. Although brought kicking and screaming into the computer age, she has mastered every new version of every new program we have ever used. As we expanded, we needed more people who knew how to design on computers, which were fast becoming the dominant tool in the burgeoning desktop publishing revolution.

Because Sharri is so great, I had no problem leaving her in charge while I spent an entire summer away at the beach with my family—Helen, Rebecca, 8, and Steven, 5—something I'd always wanted to do. It was three hours from home, but I was still going to be involved. With a laptop, a modem and a printer, I thought I could work from the beach and communicate with people over dial-up modems using a program called Timbuktu.

It sort of worked. I could receive and edit files, and I could text-message people at work and even send files to the work printers. We racked up $2,200 in long-distance charges. You pay for being an early adopter.

IT CONSTANTLY AMAZED ME how people who claimed to be experts using a Mac had only mediocre skills, the result of being mostly self-taught. One of our designers managed to avoid using the photo-cropping tool for a year because she didn't know what it was for. It became clear to me that we needed to train people how to use their computers better. I'd been teaching publication design at American University and knew I had a knack for it.

Our first AURAS training session was held in 1993 at the Four Seasons in Georgetown. It was a two-day session introducing designers and publishers to digital design and production. We gave live demonstrations and a notebook with informative booklets and programs and fonts that we had developed at AURAS. We still see those fonts pop up online every so often. The sessions went well, but the best attendee comment was that "it was the best food I'd ever had at a training session."

Because of my connection with the Art Directors Club and American University, I was asked to substitute for a speaker at a Folio:Show conference in 1992. That began a relationship with the show that lasted for 15 years (under three different owners, no less). At that time the Folio:Show, held every fall in New York, was the largest publishing conference in the country, and so popular that they added smaller annual shows in Los Angeles, D.C. and Chicago, and a second show in New York.

When I spoke in D.C., the conference director approached me and said my ideas made so much sense that Folio: ought to employ me to do its show marketing. Over the next seven years, AURAS produced Folio: materials as well as new branding and marketing programs for four other conferences, and I spoke at its conferences for eight years after that.

BY THE END OF THE DECADE, our Kalorama townhouse was getting cramped. We started looking for space in Silver Spring, both because it was near my current home, and—having grown up in Silver Spring and watched its decline during the 1980s—I wanted to do something to help revive the downtown. Plus, the real estate prices were a bargain compared to Northwest D.C.

One of the most interesting buildings in Silver Spring happened to be for sale. It was built as a Masonic Temple in 1927. The building underwent a cheap renovation in the early 1980s, and now the windows were boarded and the paint was peeling. At 12,000 square feet, it was much larger than we needed. But despite the roof leaks and dead pigeon in the top floor space, it just took one look at the views through the wrap-around windows to convince me we should be in this space.

After I called the listing agent to express interest, I immediately received three phone calls from different county and state agencies, all offering to help make the deal work. Montgomery County was anxious to get something going in downtown Silver Spring and wanted to help.

Even though a real estate agent warned it would be a tough sell at our asking price, we sold the Kalorama townhouse to the first people who looked at it, furniture and all. What sold the place to them was the modern renovation, proving that smart design has a strong return on investment. Because of the quick sale, we had to move out before our new space was finished.

In February 1998, we left our studio of nine years and rented temporary space next door to the Masons Hall. One thing that had delayed the build-out was our discovery that, hidden by the poor 1980s renovation, the original Greek Revival details of the third-floor ceremonial hall were still intact.

Our initial plan, working with architects Howard Goldstein and Jill Shick, had been a hip loft with exposed pipes and HVAC ducts, but now we decided to restore the third floor to an approximation of its initial design, with modern updates. Our builders hired a specialty firm—one that regularly worked on the U.S. Capitol—to restore the egg-and-dart molding, rosettes and the Masonic symbol itself, a three-foot plaster relief in the center of the ceiling.

We moved into 8435 Georgia Avenue, rechristened the AURAS Building, in July 1998. It was the first new building project in downtown Silver Spring in seven years. At the ribbon-cutting ceremony, attended by county and state movers-and-shakers, I said that I hoped one day soon our little building would be the least interesting thing on the intersection. That has largely become true, and I couldn't be happier.

Soon after we moved in, the Silver Spring Regional Center—the county agency tasked with reviving the downtown—brought Discovery Channel's President and CEO over to see our new space. We don't really know if it made a difference, but a week later Discovery announced it would build a new headquarters right across the street from us.

From our perch at one end of the downtown business district, we've watched a remarkable renaissance occur in an inner-suburb town center that had almost become a giant indoor mall.

We had restored the building but originally built out only the third floor for our space. Proving the old axiom that real estate is "location, location, location," Montgomery County leased the first two floors for the Silver Spring Regional Center and Urban District, which became another AURAS client.

The AURAS Building in Silver Spring, Md.

Our current space is an entire open floor surrounded by windows on all four sides.

Our routine was to have a production meeting every Tuesday morning, going over project schedules and reviewing work. That is where we were on September 11, 2001, when we heard about the terrorist attacks. Like millions of others, we spent the rest of the morning huddled together watching the tragedy unfold. We didn't know what was going to happen next, but with all of the speculation on the news and the uncertainty, we were honestly glad to be away from the center of the city.

THE EARLY 2000s were halcyon years for AURAS. We had a brand-new studio, we were producing 17 magazines, outputting film for most of them, and we were getting rent from the County on the other two floors. Maybe it was because we were doing so well that we became a little too complacent. When the Internet became a place where clients could place content, we missed the rich opportunities of being a pioneer in the emerging field of web design. Of course we eventually developed the skills to build web sites and produce media content for our clients, but the phenomenal advantage that early adopters caught by focusing on the web, echoing our own good fortune a decade earlier with personal computers, was a golden opportunity we should have exploited.

In our defense, no one knew in 2000 the far-reaching consequences that ever-expanding bandwidth would have on the graphic design business and the general cultural landscape. But one thing was clear—designing solely for print was going to be less profitable.

Another major revolution occurred at the same time. Print shops, which had been creating printing plates using negative film, discovered a new technology that would eliminate nearly all their time-consuming, labor-intensive prepress operations. Adobe's Portable Document Format (PDF), introduced in 1998, was intended to create files that would retain original formatting of documents so they could be read on a computer by anyone using its free reader software. But another use for the format was to encapsulate all the prepress information that had formerly been sent to imagesetters producing negative film for stripping. Data from PDF files could be directly scanned onto plates, eliminating film entirely.

Of course, most designers had no clue how to properly format their documents to trap ink correctly, or how to use spot colors or overprint, or how to correct color images. But we did. We'd done it for years.

In 2002 we produced 12,000 sheets of film, but in 2003 only 1,600. Printers—a notoriously conservative bunch—had adopted a PDF workflow amazingly quickly, and our days of "printing money" were over.

The first big project that we sent to the printer entirely as a digital file was a commemorative magazine for the American Chemical Society. The printer was in Florida, and we used our ISDN connection to send the 200-meg file to them in four hours. Two days later, a proof was delivered to us via FedEx. Even when we had provided negatives, it would still take a local printer four days to make proofs. These had come in a day. And they looked fabulous. It was pretty clear what the future of printing was going to be like. The critical issue from now on was how well your source file was made, because the printer wouldn't be responsible for printing mistakes caused by badly constructed files.

WE BOUGHT OUR FIRST SERIOUS transparency scanner in 1995, but it only scanned 35mm transparencies; the rest we sent to a service bureau with a big Scitex scanner. But in 1999 we bought a new, much more expensive scanner from a company called FlexTight. It could scan transparencies up to 8 x 10 at resolutions of 4000 ppi, more than enough for any image we encountered. More critical, the quality rivaled what we were getting from our outside vendor. AURAS became capable of producing every part of a print product at high quality completely in-house.

It was such a great scanner, we paid it off in six months and ultimately bought another. But scanning transparencies was soon ending, too, as serious digital cameras began replacing film. By the mid-2000s we began seeing more and more digital files and had far fewer transparencies to scan.

EVERY BUSINESS HAS ITS UPS AND DOWNS, but AURAS had always done better year by year. In 2006, we were 25 years old, and felt pretty impervious to the economy. Revenue sources came and went. We made money outputting film and scanning transparencies, but even when technologies changed, we were still producing magazines, marketing materials and identity programs, and working on our most ambitious product ever—producing our own magazine, which launched in 2007.

So it came as a complete surprise that when the economy tanked in late 2007, it took many of our clients down, too. By 2009, we were producing half the magazines we had in 2005. For the first time in our history, I reluctantly had to let people go.

So maybe 2007 was a bad time to introduce *FPO—For Publications Only*. It was an extension of the newsletters we had been producing since 2004 and the classes we had been teaching for nearly as long.

The author at his usual post, hand on trackball, at his typically messy desk.

Magazine design, editing and production was something we knew a lot about, and we knew a lot of people who could use a magazine about it.

The business plan was pretty realistic; we needed at least 2,500 subscriptions to start, and we figured that it should be a breeze to find them. Since *Print* had 30,000 subscribers and *HOW* had 24,000, we should be able to get 5 percent of them interested in another magazine. That was the theory, anyway.

To be generous, let's call *FPO* a cult favorite. Readers liked the magazine and got a lot from it, but as the recession deepened, we ran out of money to promote the magazine. We had been hoping the magazine would get some Internet viral boost to help it grow, but that wasn't happening. And boy, the *schadenfreude* that comes with producing a magazine in your own field is kind of awesome. Everyone thinks they know more than you do, and no one is slow to point out your mistakes. We have produced seven issues to date and hope to do more occasionally.

WHERE ARE WE NOW that we have reached our 30th year? The magazine business is in turmoil, faced with new delivery methods, new technologies and huge competition from media platforms that were not even imagined three decades ago. Whether it's remaking print publications for an iPad or developing Web sites using HTML5 or Flash to deliver a graphic experience that can rival print design (but with the added capability of motion, sound and interactivity)—someone *still* has to design these things.

As the years have gone by, we've become more interested in advancing the editorial message no matter what the ultimate platform, and often the best solution is a combination of print, web and social media. We have adapted by learning new skills and finding new markets. It's still fun to come to work every day, and I think the feeling is shared by Sharri Wolfgang (25 years), David Fox (16 years) and Melissa Kelly (11 years), who have come to appreciate the AURAS way of working—if not necessarily the strong coffee. Past long-term employees like Jason Clarke (10 years), Mark Colliton (8 years) and Ted Bonar (9 years) helped make the studio successful in recent years, and, more importantly, a place to enjoy work with a minimum of drama. To some degree, we have become spoiled, expecting people to like AURAS and want to stay.

Both the design of the space and the culture of the business have always been important to me. Most people are lucky to be able to create a place that represents their ideal environment; I have been fortunate to have created *two* spaces.

I have always loved the moment when a newly printed piece has been delivered. Seeing your work finally produced is always exciting. For me, it's not just visual, but tactile and even sensual. I confess to still burying my nose in a brand new publication to get a whiff of the inks and varnishes and smells of the pressroom I remember so well from my earliest experiences at Colortone. Somehow, sniffing a monitor or digital tablet just isn't the same.

ROBERT SUGAR
OCTOBER 2011
ROBSUGAR@AURAS.COM
WWW.AURAS.COM

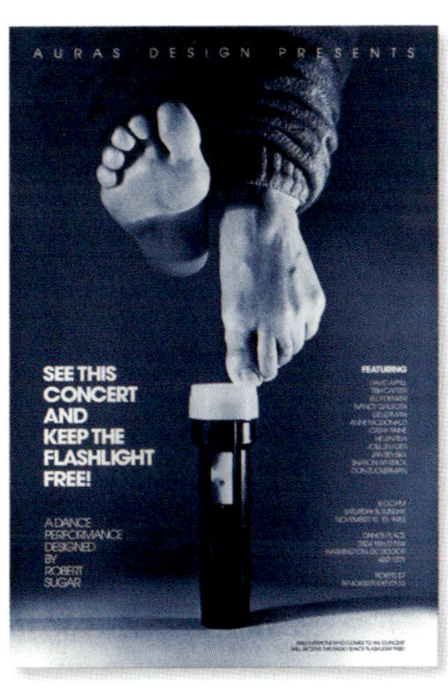

Over the years, AURAS has produced a variety of creative promotions and products: an actual modern dance concert; a funky rubber stamp set designed by Marty Ittner; and note cards that celebrate the seasons designed by Sharri Wolfgang. But our most ambitious project has been *FPO Magazine*. We have poured everything we know and love about publication design into its issues.

30 Years / 30 Clients

AURAS has had more than 200 clients over three decades. These are some of our most interesting and important projects.

1. Ancestry.com
2. American Association of Motor Vehicle Administrators
3. American Bus Association
4. American Chemical Society
5. Audio Description Associates
6. Axent Realty
7. Biblical Archaeology Society
8. Boy Scouts of America
9. Clear Connection
10. Congressional Quarterly
11. Cowles Business Media
12. Electric Cooperatives of South Carolina
13. George Washington University
14. InfoComm
15. Jewish Educational Ventures
16. Johns Hopkins School of Advanced International Studies
17. Kennedy Center
18. University of Maryland
19. Montgomery County Government
20. National Public Radio
21. National Science Teachers Association
22. Organization for the Promotion and Advancement of Small Telecommunications Companies
23. Population Action International
24. Share Our Strength
25. St. Albans School
26. Telecommunications Industry of America
27. The Rosen Group
28. Urban Land Institute
29. Washington DC Dance Coalition
30. World Bank

1

2

3

5

6

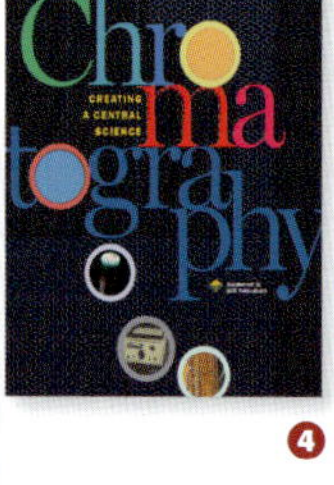

4

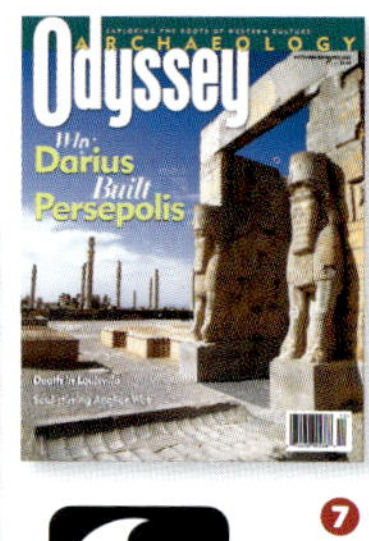

Biblical Archaeology Review

7

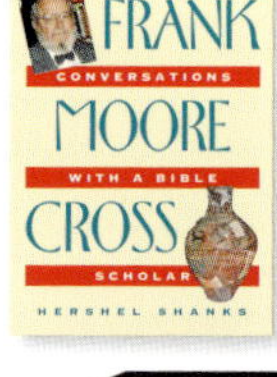

8

9

10

11

12

GSPM
THE GRADUATE SCHOOL OF POLITICAL MANAGEMENT

13

14

15

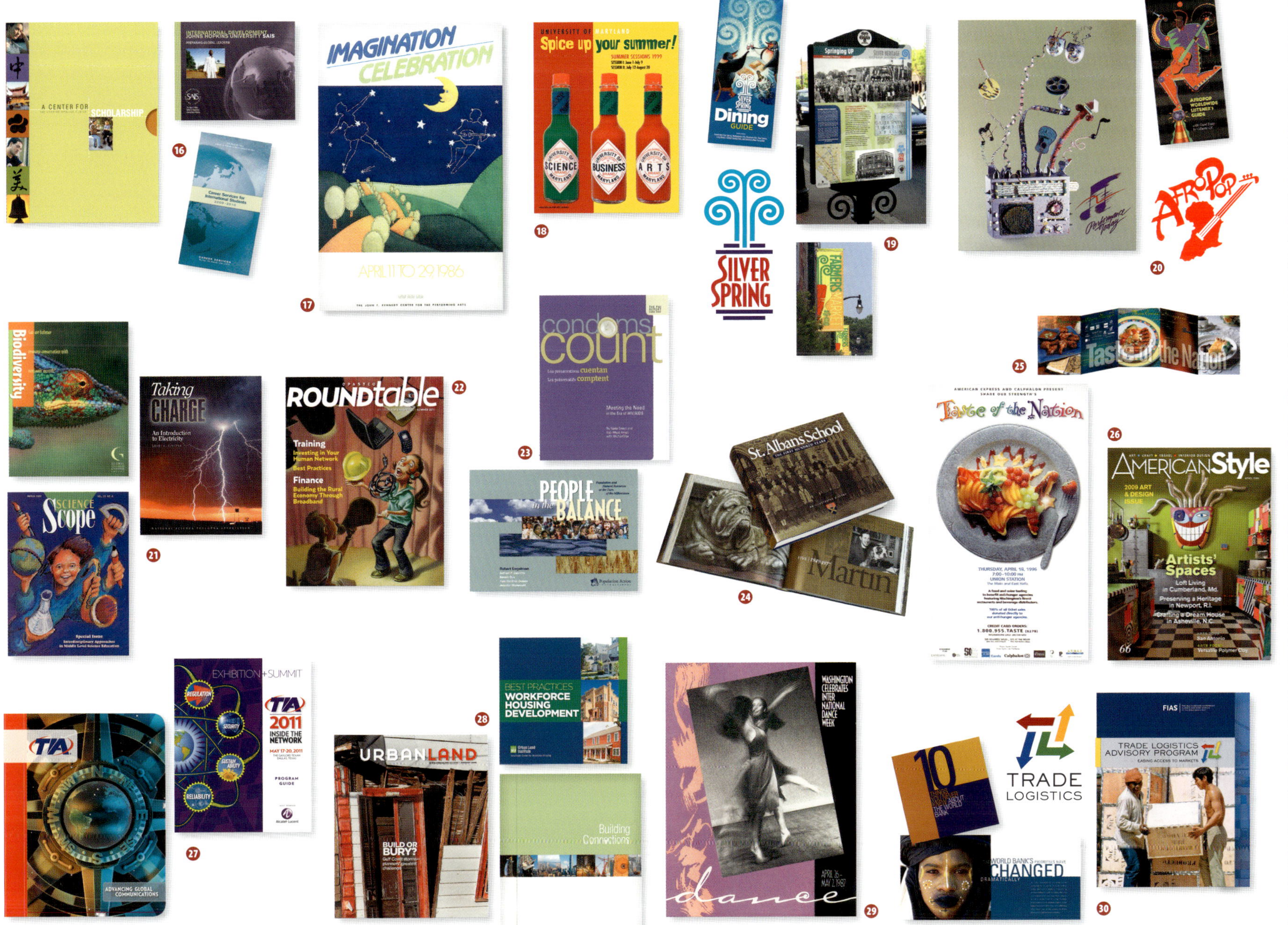
16
17
IMAGINATION CELEBRATION
APRIL 11 TO 29 1986
18
Spice up your summer!
SCIENCE
BUSINESS
ARTS
19
Dining GUIDE
SILVER SPRING
20
21
Biodiversity
Taking CHARGE
An Introduction to Electricity
Science Scope
22
ROUNDtable
23
condoms count
24
St. Albans School
25
26
Taste of the Nation
AMERICAN Style
Artists' Spaces
PEOPLE in the BALANCE
27
EXHIBITION+SUMMIT
TIA 2011
INSIDE THE NETWORK
28
URBANLAND
BUILD OR BURY?
BEST PRACTICES
WORKFORCE HOUSING DEVELOPMENT
Building Connections
29
dance
30
TRADE LOGISTICS
TRADE LOGISTICS ADVISORY PROGRAM
CHANGED

AURAS Employees

(In roughly reverse chronological order. People with five or more years at AURAS are highlighted in red.)

Robert Sugar
Helen Rea
Sharri Wolfgang
David Fox
Melissa Kelly
Andrew Chapman
Jason Clarke
Jinna Hagerty
Nancy McKeithen
Tanya Nuchols
Jeff Roberts
Chris Komisar
Ted Bonar
Dan Stump
Daryl Wakeley
Vivian Moritz
Maureen Gregory
Mark Colliton
Elyse Greer
Cynthia Eyring
Elizabeth McNulty
Ron Melé
Jake Watling
Jessie Despard
Stuart Greenwell
Scott Crawford
Catherine Garcia
Kay Irannejad
Robin Cather
Sharon Eppler
Terry Cohen
Dan Banks
JoAnne DiGeorgio
Philip Gerlach
Stacy Dadonna
Ted Smith
Marty Ittner
Debbie Bates
Ellen Baker Smyth
Valerie Weiner
Malcolm McGaughy
Evelyn Powers
Karol Keane
Sylvie Abecassis
Jane Winter
John Hannafan
Kyong Cho
Mariann Seriff

Biographies

ROBERT SUGAR

IS FOUNDER AND CREATIVE DIRECTOR OF AURAS DESIGN, a design studio that brings editorial-oriented solutions to clients' design problems.

He started AURAS Design while still enrolled at American University, where he was editor of the school yearbook and literary magazine. The studio's official start date in 1981 marked the first separate studio space for the company.

Rob taught at American University for nine years as an adjunct faculty member in the Art and Communications departments of the School of Communication.

As a pioneer in the adoption of desktop publishing tools for professional design and production of print materials, he was responsible for helping other studios and printers adopt new workflows using the technologies.

Rob has taught sessions at Folio:Show for 20 years, as well as at many other industry events, and serves as a consultant for publishers.

In 2008 he started *FPO Magazine*, a publication for editorial designers. His most ambitious work to date, however, has been his collaboration with his wife, Helen Rea, in the production of their children, Rebecca and Steven.

RENÉE COMET

IS A NOTED ADVERTISING PHOTOGRAPHER specializing in food and still-life photography. Whatever the subject, her visual treatment can best be described as uncomplicated, fluid, and elegant.

Great food should be shot big and needs a thousand and one details to be perfect. It needs to completely overtake your gaze, mesmerize you until you're hungry.

For over a quarter century, Renee's been exploring and succeeding in coercing those details into the best food photography for her clients. Each assignment is an opportunity to interpret, reinterpret, and reinvent the image to produce stunning results for her clients and collaborators. Whether it's spices for McCormick Spice or spices as healing herbs for *AARP Magazine*, or spices as ingredients for one of the thousands of recipes in the many cookbooks she's illustrated, each is an opportunity to see anew.

How each specific recipe looks best is Renee's singular goal. She focuses on conveying that decisive image: the steam, the water droplets, the light touch of sauce on the end of the fork, the moist food, the glare on the food in exactly the right place.

You can see more of Renée Comet's work, and reach her, at www.cometphoto.com.

LISA CHERKASKY

IS THE D.C. AREA'S MOST SOUGHT-AFTER FOOD STYLIST. She brings a rare skill, creativity, and flair to all her work. A graduate of the Culinary Institute of America, Lisa has been working in the world of food for more than 35 years—cooking in restaurants as both a chef and pastry chef, writing, catering, teaching, styling, and eating.

She has been independently employed for more than 25 years and counts among her clients McCormick Spice, *The Washington Post*, Marble Slab Ice Cream, Mount Vernon, Monticello, the Smithsonian, Zatarain's, Meat and Livestock Australia, and National Geographic.

You can find Lisa on her website, www.LisaCherkasky.com, and also writing and riffing on sandwiches at www.TheLunchEncounter.com.